THE COMPLETE PRESCHOOL PROGRAM

Arlene L. Martin

Learning Publications, Inc.

Holmes Beach, Florida

Copyright 1987 by **Arlene L. Martin**

All rights reserved. No part of this book may be reproduced or transmitted in any form or by any means, electronic or mechanical, including photocopying and recording, or by any information or retrieval system, without permission in writing from the publisher.

Learning Publications, Inc.
P.O. Box 1326, 5351 Gulf Drive
Holmes Beach, Florida 34217

ISBN 155691-008-8

Cover Design by Jim Harris

Printing: 1 2 3 4 5 6 7 8 9   Year: 7 8 9 0 1 2

ACKNOWLEDGEMENTS

My greatest gratitude goes to my husband Jim, who gave much moral support and confidence. He also edited the rough drafts which took a great amount of objectivity and kindness.

There are others who reviewed this material, gave encouragement, and/or made valuable suggestions. Thank you to Danna Downing, Diane Vitek, Dr. Mary Cain, Sharon Ansell, Laurie Bowersox, and Laura Shaw.

Much appreciation goes to Karen Jacobsen and the staff of Learning Publications for all their efforts in making it possible for me to share these ideas with many.

TABLE OF CONTENTS

Introduction 1

Chapter 1–Daily Basics 3

    A.   Daily Schedule 3
    B.   Daily Tasks 4

Chapter 2–Daily Lesson Plans 11

DLP 1	School Acquaintance	11
DLP 2-7	Self-Awareness	12
DLP 8-17	Fall	18
DLP 18	Explorers	28
DLP 19-22	Shapes	29
DLP 23-31	Winter	34
DLP 32-33	Jobs	43
DLP 34	Peace	45
DLP 35-36	Senses	47
DLP 37	Family	50
DLP 38	Address	51
DLP 39	Telephone	52
DLP 40-42	Valentine's Day	53
DLP 43	Patriotic Holidays	56
DLP 44-45	Transportation	57
DLP 46-47	Health	59
DLP 48	Special Holidays	61
DLP 49-54	Spring	62
DLP 55	Day and Night	68
DLP 56-58	Farm	69
DLP 59	Zoo Animals	73
DLP 60	May Day	74
DLP 61	Special Family Days	75
DLP 62	Natural Environment	76
DLP 63-64	Plants	77
DLP 65-67	Music	79

Chapter 3–Curriculum Aids 83

    A.   Alphabet Train 83
    B.   Color Wheel 83
    C.   Days of the Week Chart 84
    D.   Height Chart 84
    E.   Pocket Chart 84
    F.   Weather Chart 85
    G.   Sequence of Days Chart 86
    H.   Initial Sound Cards 89
    I.   Rhyming Word Cards 94

Chapter 4–Curriculum Activity Selections 97

    A.   Free Play Activities 97
          1.   Special Free Play Activities 100
              a.   Alphabet Book 100
              b.   Book of Colors 100
              c.   Numeral Book of Tiny Things 101
              d.   Book of Feelings 101
    B.   Songs 101
    C.   Fingerplays 103
    D.   Nutritious Snacks 112
    E.   Science Experiences 113
    F.   Games 117
    G.   Field Trips 119
    H.   Bulletin Board Ideas 119

Chapter 5–Program Management Aids 123

    A.   Checklists 123
          1.   Intellectual/Physical Development 123
          2.   Checklist of Observations. 129
          3.   Year End Report 130
    B.   Record Keeping 133
          1.   Child Information Form 133
          2.   Anecdotal Record Form 135
          3.   Attendance Charts. 135
          4.   Individual Child File Folder. 136
          5.   Resource Files 136
              a.   Theme-Related Files. 136
              b.   General Files 136
    C.   Home/School Interactions 137
          1.   Parental Involvement in the Preschool Program 137
          2.   Preschool Preparation 137
          3.   Questionnaire. 138
          4.   Learning Fun At Home 140
    D.   Operating Expenses 143

INTRODUCTION

The Complete Preschool Program contains, in five chapters, the information necessary for a teacher to manage a preschool class. Its 67 Daily Lesson Plans present a comprehensive guide for preschool teachers at every level of experience. For those who are beginning their teaching careers, the book provides an easy-to-follow program that is ready for immediate use. Conversely, for those teachers in schools with already well-developed curricula, *The Complete Preschool Program* offers many fresh ideas and activities suitable for integration into their already existing programs.

Chapter 1, **Daily Basics**, presents a recommended model for a preschool daily schedule, along with a task-by-task description of responsibilities for the Teacher, the Teacher's Assistant, and the Children, during a typical preschool day.

Chapter 2, **Daily Lesson Plans**, consists of 67 theme-related lesson plans. Complete in themselves, the plans are also meant to serve as models for teachers to use in creating other, more personalized plan variations.

Chapter 3, **Curriculum Aids**, contains a variety of Classroom Charts and Lesson Cards which are frequently referred to for use in many of the Daily Lesson Plans.

Chapter 4, **Curriculum Activity Selections**, provides an informed sampling of ready-to-use ideas for teachers to customize and incorporate into the Daily Lesson Plans.

Chapter 5, **Program Management Aids**, treats a variety of typical school management considerations and provides models for dealing with critical organizational needs. The chapter's checklists, forms and guidelines are designed to provide criteria and documents on which to record assessments of the children's skills and progress. The section on Home/School Interaction contains specific recommendations to facilitate harmonious and productive relations among the school staff, the children and their parents.

Working with children is a rewarding adventure. *The Complete Preschool Program* is meant to be a stimulating and pragmatic guide for that adventure.

1

DAILY BASICS

Effective and efficient preschool teaching requires extremely careful planning and execution. An essential component for achieving success is the design of a workable daily schedule.

A. THE DAILY SCHEDULE

The daily schedule (as shown in the following chart) represents the activities to be presented in 2 3/4 hours of class time. However, the schedule can be adjusted to fit any time frame. While the amount of time to be allotted for each activity is not a fixed quantity, a daily sequence of activities should be established and should remain the same, as much as possible, throughout the school year. This consistency will allow the children to know what to expect during each day.

[Note: The activities in the following schedule correspond to those in each of the 67 Daily Lesson Plans in Chapter II.]

DAILY SCHEDULE CHART

1. Pre-Class Preparation	Time as needed
2. Daily Elements	**Approximate Time**
a. Free Play	40 minutes
b. Lesson Skill 1	15 minutes
Lesson Skill 2	15 minutes
c. Handwork	15 minutes
d. Clean Up	10 minutes
e. Pre-Story	15 minutes
f. Story Time	15 minutes
g. Dismiss Group	2 minutes
h. Snack	13 minutes
i. Science Experience	5 minutes
j. Outside and/or Game	15 minutes
k. Discuss Activities of the Day	5 minutes
l. Prepare to Leave	Time as needed
m. Dismissal	Time as needed
3. After Class	Time as needed

B. THE DAILY TASKS

The following are the daily tasks to be undertaken by the Teacher, the Teacher's Assistant and the Children, before, during and after a typical preschool day.

1. Pre-Class Preparation

Careful pre-class preparation is a necessity which delivers many practical results. Most important, it allows the Teacher and the Teacher's Assistant to make the most productive use of every moment with the children. During pre-class preparation:

The Teacher:

* previews the Daily Lesson Plan to determine what has to be done and which materials are needed.

* lists jobs and sets out materials for the Teacher's Assistant.

* fills in a Daily Jobs form (see below) for self and for Teacher's Assistant.

```
==============================================================
                        Daily Jobs
==============================================================
    Date              Job 1                    Job 2

    9/10           Lesson #1            "All About Me" book
    Tues.      Present Tense Verbs          Hand Prints
==============================================================

        Danny     _____
        Jenni     _____
        Craig     _____
        Becki     _____
        Carlos    _____
        Doug      _____
        Brian     _____
        Larry     _____
        Dasika    _____
        Katie     _____
        Jamie     _____
        Patrick   _____
        Rachel    _____

==============================================================
```

For convenience and efficiency, the Teacher should design and duplicate a Daily Jobs form for daily use. In addition to listing all of the children's names, the form should have a space for the date and sufficient job description column spaces to accommodate all of each day's jobs. The Daily Jobs form is a reminder to note every child's performance each day and provides valuable information for later transfer to the children's permanent records. Both Teacher and Teacher's Assistant keep Daily Jobs forms with them to use as they work with the children.

Daily Basics

2. Throughout The Day

The Teacher:

* announces transitions from one activity to another approximately five minutes before they occur. (This will allow the children to end one project and prepare for the next.)

* displays the next appropriate Sequence of Day Card, as sequence change announcements are made.

The Teacher's Assistant:

* prepares materials for the following day(s), as time permits.

a. Free Play Activity

==

Depending on the availability of supplies and equipment, free play activities may include:

coloring	puzzles	small blocks
painting	clay or play dough	large blocks
cutting	table games	woodworking area
pasting	books	housekeeping area
collage work	manipulative toys	sand table
interest center	science table	

==

[See Chapter IV for specific Free Play Activity suggestions.]

The Teacher:

* greets the children.

* allows the children to choose their own activities or, if they are hesitant or unfamiliar with what is available, guides them to an activity.

* visits with the children as they are playing.

* monitors their actions and behaviors, as necessary.

* leads planned activities.

The Teacher's Assistant:

* prepares for upcoming activities, as indicated by the Teacher and/or the Daily Lesson Plan.

* assists children as needed.

The Children:

* involve themselves in the Free Play activities of their choice or in planned activities led by the Teacher. (Participation in planned activities is optional.)

b. **Lesson Skill**

[Note: Each of the Daily Lesson Plans (DLP) contains two Lesson Skills. The second Lesson Skill in each plan recurs three times throughout the entire course of the 67 DLP's (to show the children's progress at each of three stages.]

The Teacher:

* works with the children on Lesson Skill objectives as indicated in the Daily Lesson Plans. Though some Lesson Skills will involve the entire group, most are designed as small group or individual activities. Therefore, it may be necessary to start working with one or more of the children during Free Play. (The best time to interrupt is when a child has finished one Free Play activity but hasn't started another.) Let the child know that he or she is needed for a special purpose. Also, assure the child that afterwards he or she will be able to return to more Free Play activity.

* During the Lesson Skill activity, makes notes on the daily job checklist about the performance of each child. The lessons require a wide range of maturity levels in many areas. Therefore, the Teacher always lets the children do as much as they can on their own, only helping them with tasks that are truly beyond their capabilities, to keep them from becoming discouraged; also, always praises their accomplishments.

The Teacher's Assistant:

* works with the children on the Lesson Skills, as indicated by the teacher or assists the children who are not involved in working with the teacher on a lesson.

The Children:

* listen to and respond to the Teacher.

c. **Handwork**

The Teacher:

* explains the day's project and helps the children only as necessary.

The Teacher's Assistant:

* assists as needed.

The Children:

* use a variety of materials and methods as presented by the teacher. (Handwork activities present multiple opportunities for developing their fine motor skills and for observing many different ways to put things together.)

Daily Basics

d. **Clean Up**

The Teacher:

* helps all of the children to be involved in this activity by guiding them to areas where things need to be put away, and by explaining and showing them exactly what to do, if necessary.

The Teacher's Assistant:

* also guides the children.

The Children:

* put things away.

e. **Pre-story**

The Teacher:

* leads the following activities:

    —Weather Chart and Days of Week Chart [See Chapter III.]

    —Sharing Time provides children with an opportunity to tell of a significant experience or possession. (It may be necessary to assign a "Sharing Time" day to a few children each day. Then, all will have the experience, and the other children will not become restless from hearing too many presentations in a single day.)

    —Songs and Fingerplays [See Chapter IV.]

The Teacher's Assistant:

* gets the snack ready and then prepares materials for the following day(s).

The Children:

* participate in each activity.

f. **Story**

The Teacher:

* makes the story time interesting by reading stories and books that capture the attention of the children, including their personal favorites, those that they bring to school, and books related to the theme of the Daily Lesson Plan.

* uses puppets, flannel graphs, filmstrips, videotapes, and other audiovisual materials to add variety. (AV programs and playback devices often can be borrowed from the public library, if not available at school).

The Teacher's Assistant:

* continues with the same tasks as in Pre-story. (However, if a child is having trouble sitting and listening, the Teacher's Assistant may need to sit by the child. If that does not work, the Teacher's Assistant takes the child to an area where the child will not be a distraction and where the Teacher's Assistant can attend to another task.)

The Children:

* learn to listen and sit quietly for a short time.

g. **Dismiss Group Activity**

The Teacher:

* dismisses the children to the snack table, individually or in groups, according to a variety of classification activities (see the DLP's for examples). The activities are designed to teach self-awareness and promote orderly behavior.

The Teacher's Assistant:

* assists as needed.

The Children:

* listen to the teacher to hear and understand the classification clues that indicate their turns to go to the snack table.

h. **Snack**

[See Chapter IV for nutritious snack suggestions.]

The Teacher:

* brings the snack to the table with the help of one child.

* has relaxed, spontaneous conversations with the children.

The Teacher's Assistant:

* assists as needed.

The Children:

* take turns helping the Teacher to pass out the snack. (Helping allows each child an opportunity to behave responsibly and enables the child to learn one-to-one correspondence while giving snacks to classmates.)

Daily Basics

- * quietly visit and enjoy being together.
- * dispose of their own cups, napkins and leftovers in the proper places.

i. **Science Experience**

[See Chapter IV for specific Science Experiences.]

The Teacher:

- * presents the materials and procedures in the Science Experience.
- * promotes the children's active involvement in the activities.

The Teacher's Assistant:

- * assists as needed.

The Children:

- * participate in the science activities as directed by the teacher.

j. **Outside Activities and/or Games**

[See Chapter IV for specific games.]

The Teacher:

- * monitors the children and promotes safe play, inside or out.
- * in inclement weather, organizes inside active play, such as using gymnastic equipment, marching with rhythm instruments or playing games.

[Note: Most inside activities listed in the DLP can be conducted outside in good weather.]

The Teacher's Assistant:

- * cleans up the classroom.
- * sorts the children's class work into individual piles ready to be taken home. Includes with these, Learning Fun at Home activities (see Chapter V) as suggested by Teacher.

The Children:

- * play outside on playground equipment.
- * take nature walks.

* play games.

* in inclement weather, are involved in active play as determined by the teacher.

k. **Discuss the Activities of the Day**

The Teacher:

* helps the children to recall the activities of the day by using questions or leading statements, as needed, to encourage all of the children to contribute.

* uses a tape recorder (so the children can hear themselves), or draws simple pictures to depict the activities that the children mention. (The tape recorder and drawings will help the children to remember their school activities.)

The Teacher's Assistant:

* continues with the same tasks as in the previous time period.

The Children:

* review the day's activities and share their thoughts with their classmates.

l. **Prepare to Leave**

The Teacher:

* assists in helping the children to dress, when necessary.

* distributes class work, notices or other materials to be taken home by the children (includes "Learning Fun at Home" notes.)

* gives each child a personalized "Good-bye!"

* talks to the parents about any problems or commendable behavior.

The Teacher's Assistant:

* helps the children to get dressed when necessary.

* distributes class work, notices and other materials.

The Children:

* put on their outside clothing.

* gather their finished work and notes.

* leave when their rides arrive.

2

DAILY LESSON PLANS

DAILY LESSON PLAN 1

Theme: School Acquaintance

- Free Play

Special Activity A: My School Room

Procedure: Encourage the children to become familiar with the room.

Special Activity B: Height/Weight

Procedure: Record each child's height on the Height Chart. Also, record the date and each child's weight on his/her Anecdotal Record Sheet. [See Table of Contents for pages.]

Lesson Skill 15: Language Development

Objective: To increase vocabulary by naming classroom objects

Materials: An assortment of individual classroom objects, such as a crayon, a pair of scissors, a pencil, an eraser, a toy truck, a book, a block, a doll, a stick of chalk, a ball, and others

Procedure: Have each child choose one object from the group and say, "This is a/an _____." Then he/she returns the objects to their proper places in the room, (if able).

Lesson Skill 77a: Gross Motor Coordination

Objective: To improve large muscle abilities by running, skipping, jumping, hopping

Procedure: Have each child run, skip, jump and hop to the Teacher from a designated point. Note and record the child's coordination. (May be done during "Outside" time.)

Handwork: Sandpaper Crayon Melt

Materials: Crayons, white paper, iron, ironing board or heavy cloth, the first letter of each child's name cut out of sandpaper (rough side shows the letter backwards)

Procedure: Have each child color his/her first initial on its rough side. Then, as the children watch, iron the sandpaper initials (colored sides down) onto separate pieces of white paper.

- Clean Up

- Pre-Story Activities: Weather, Days of Week, Songs, Fingerplays, Sharing Time

Special Activity C: Classroom Rules

Procedure: Discuss classroom rules with the children:
1) Be careful not to hurt anyone.
2) Use objects with care.

Special Activity D: Sequence of Day Cards

Procedure: Discuss the Sequence of Day cards. [See Table of Contents.] Explain their significance.

- Story

- Dismiss Group Procedure: Dismiss one or two children at a time, good listeners first. Have them jump to the snack table.

- Snack

- Science Experience

- Outside Activities and/or Games

Special Activity E: Photo Session

Procedure: Encourage the children to explore the outdoor equipment. Take a photograph of each child (for use in Daily Lesson Plan 4).

- Discuss Activities of the Day

- Prepare to Leave / Dismissal

DAILY LESSON PLAN 2

Theme: Self-Awareness

Lesson Skill 19: Language Development

Objective: To increase vocabulary by naming articles of clothing

Materials: A box containing articles of clothing and other objects

Procedure: Tell the children that there are clothes and other objects in the box. Have each child, in turn, pick out an article of clothing and tell what it is: "This is a/an _____." (May be done during Pre-Story Activities time.)

Lesson Skill 88a: Visual Motor Coordination

Objective: To improve eye-hand coordination by drawing a person

Materials: Chalkboard, chalk, paper, crayons

Procedure: Draw a picture of a person on the chalkboard as the children suggest body parts. Then have each child draw a picture of a person as completely as he/she possibly can. Write each child's name and the date on his/her paper. File the drawings in the child's individual file folder.

- Handwork: Puppets

Materials: Felt markers, pre-sewn cloth puppets

Procedure: Using felt markers, have each child draw a person on the pre-sewn cloth puppets. Show the children how to use the puppets and give them time to do so.

- Clean Up

- Pre-Story Activities: Weather, Days of Week, Songs, Fingerplays, Sharing Time

- Story

- Dismiss Group Procedure: Describe each child. A child who thinks he or she is being described stands up and goes to the snack table, if the description fits.

- Snack

- Science Experience

- Outside Activities and/or Games

- Discuss Activities of the Day

- Prepare to Leave / Dismissal

DAILY LESSON PLAN 3

Theme: Self-Awareness

- Free Play

Lesson Skill 13: Language Development

Objective: To construct sentences using conjunctions

Procedure: Lead the children in a series of body movements. Then ask one child to identify the last two movements that the group was doing. (Example: hopping and jumping). Use the action verbs said by the child in a sentence containing a conjunction. (Example: We were hopping and jumping.) Have the child repeat the sentence. Then have all of the children repeat the sentence while doing the actions. Continue performing the same two actions, until every child has had a chance to say the sentence containing the conjunction. Use combinations of other action verbs to form sentences which make use of all three conjunctions: and, but and or. Have the children say those sentences, too.

Sentence examples: We jump and hop. We nodded our heads but did not snap our fingers. I can hop on my right foot or on my left foot. We can smile or frown with our mouths. (May be done during Pre-Story time.)

Lesson Skill 43a: Memory

Objective: To recall data necessary to name body parts

Materials: Mirror, paper, pencil

Procedure: Work with the children individually. Have each child name as many of his/her body parts as possible. For clarity and reinforcement, try using a large mirror in which both teacher and child can point out and see the various parts. Record the date and the body parts that each child names. File the list in the child's individual file folder (for a progress comparison later in the year).

- Handwork: Wooden Spoon Dolls

Materials: Felt markers, yarn, flat wooden spoons (may be available at ice cream stores or in the dairy section of grocery stores; plastic spoons or tongue depressors may be substituted)

Procedure: Have the children draw faces on the wooden spoons and tie yarn bows around the handles of their spoons. (Help tie bows where necessary.)

- Clean Up

- Pre-Story Activities: Weather, Days of Week, Songs, Fingerplays, Sharing Time

- Story

- Dismiss Group Procedure: Notice and name the color of each child's eyes. Then dismiss the children in groups as they recognize the name of the color that matches their eyes.

- Snack

- Science Experience

- Outside Activities and/or Games

- Discuss Activities of the Day

- Prepare to Leave / Dismissal

DAILY LESSON PLAN 4

Theme: Self-Awareness

- Free Play

<u>Special Activity A:</u> Covers for "All About Me" Books [See DLP 4 - 7 for directions for making entire book.]

Materials: Colored construction paper sheets (8 1/2" x 11"), marking pens

Procedure: (Write "All About Me" at the top and "By _____" on each paper sheet for front cover.) Have each child draw a picture of himself/herself on the front cover and sign his/her name in the blank space after the word "By _____". (Give help with writing names, as needed.)

Lesson Skill 8: Language Development

Objective: To construct sentences using the possessive forms of names

Materials: A photo of each child (made in Daily Lesson Plan 1) and a Pocket Chart. [See Table of Contents.]

Procedure: Place all of the photos on the pocket chart. Have all of the children meet as a group. Then, one at a time, have the children choose someone else's picture from the pocket chart. Each child should identify the person in the picture by saying, for example, "This is Danny's picture," and then hand the picture to the teacher. Continue until all of the children have used the possessive form of a proper name in a sentence.

Lesson Skill 78a: Gross Motor Coordination

Objective: To improve large muscle abilities by throwing and catching a ball

Materials: A ball, 8" or larger

Procedure: From a distance of 4 to 8 feet, have each child throw the ball to the teacher and then catch it. Repeat the exchange several times to determine the child's level of skill (and to have fun). Record the level for the child's individual file. (May be done during "Outside" time.)

- Handwork: "All About Me" Book — Pages 1 and 2 [See DLP 4-7 for directions for the entire book.]

Page 1: "Photo"

Materials: Photo of each child (from Daily Lesson Plan 1), markers, photo triangles, 8 1/2 x 11" paper

Procedure: Demonstrate the use of the triangles. Then have each child attach his/her photo to the upper half of the paper. Next, have each child write as much of his/her name as possible under the photograph.

Page 2: "Initial"

Materials: Glue, scissors, a 6" initial of each child's first name pre-drawn on construction paper, additional sheets of construction paper (8 1/2 x 11")

Procedure: Have each child cut out his/her first name initial and glue it on the paper. Write "This is the first letter of my name" at the bottom of their pages.

- Clean Up

- Pre-Story Activities: Weather, Days of Week, Songs, Fingerplays, Sharing Time

<u>Special Activity B:</u> The "All About Me" Book

Procedure: Remind children about the "All About Me" book. Explain that the pages must be left at school for a few more days. If time permits, show the children's already completed pages.

- Story

- Dismiss Group Procedure: Show all of the completed Page 1 photo pages. Dismiss each child as he/she recognizes his/her photo. As the child goes to the snack table, say, "This is _____'s picture," using the possessive form of the child"s name.

- Snack

- Science Experience

- Outside Activities and/or Games

- Discuss Activities of the Day

- Prepare to Leave / Dismissal

Daily Lesson Plans

DAILY LESSON PLAN 5

Theme: Self-Awareness

- Free Play

Special Activity A: "Alphabet Book" — Letter "A" [See Table of Contents.]

Lesson Skill 48: Math Readiness

Objective: To establish a basis for understanding math by sorting objects

Materials: Chalk, crayons, pencils, toy farm animals, toy people, balls, spoons

Procedure: Working with each child individually, ask him/her to sort the objects into groups according to their similarities. If the child does not know what to do, start by selecting one object from each group. Then ask him/her to match the selected objects with others of a similar nature.

Lesson Skill 42a: Memory

Objective: To recall data necessary to name colors

Materials: Color Wheel

Procedure: Working with each child individually, point to the colors on the color wheel. Ask the child to identify the colors. Record any unfamiliar colors. Help the child to learn one or two new colors in reference to colored objects in the room.

- Handwork: "All About Me" Book — Pages 3 and 4 [Book completed in DLP 4-7]

Page 3: "Age"

Materials: 8 1/2 x 11" paper, pre-drawn birthday cakes and pre-cut construction paper candles, marker pens or crayons and scissors

Procedure: Have each child cut out a birthday cake and glue it onto a piece of paper. Next, have him/her choose as many candles as his/her age in years and glue them on top of the cake. (The children may want to decorate their cakes with pens or crayons.) At the bottom of each paper, write, "I am ___ years old." Ask each child's age and write it in the blank.

Page 4: "Favorite Color"

Materials: Crayons, a picture of a crayon (drawn on 8 1/2 x 11" paper)

Procedure: Have each child color a picture of a crayon with his/her favorite color. Write "My favorite color is ___." at the bottom of each page. Ask the child to identify the color of his/her crayon. Then write the color's name in the blank.

- Clean Up

- Pre-Story Activities: Weather, Days of Week, Songs, Fingerplays, Sharing Time

Special Activity B: "All About Me" Book

Procedure: Show and read the completed pages of the "All About Me" books.

Special Activity C: "Alphabet Book"

Procedure: Discuss the "Alphabet Book," pointing out that there will be a page for each letter in the alphabet. Show all the letters and explain that it will take many school days to finish this book.

Special Activity D: "Alphabet Train" — Letter "A" [See Table of Contents.]

- Story

- Dismiss Group Procedure: Dismiss children by their clothing color. Say, for example, "If you are wearing something green, you may go to the snack table."

- Snack

- Science Experience

- Outside Activities and/or Games

- Discuss Activities of the Day

- Prepare to Leave / Dismissal

DAILY LESSON PLAN 6

Theme: Self-Awareness

- Free Play

Special Activity A: "Alphabet Book"—Letter "B"
[See Table of Contents.]

Special Activity B: "All About Me" Book

Page 9: "My Handprint"

Materials: 8 1/2" x 11" paper, a crayon

Procedure: Draw an outline around each child's hand on 8 1/2 x 11" paper and write "My Handprint" at the bottom of each page.

Lesson Skill 7: Language Development

Objective: To construct sentences using plural inflections

Materials: Food such as popcorn, raisins, crackers, peanuts, jelly beans, cold cereal and others

Procedure: Working with each child individually, put a raisin on the table and say, "Here is one raisin." Then put another raisin next to the first one and say, "Now there are two of them. There are two of what?" The child answers, "There are two raisins." Repeat the pattern with two or three other objects.

Lesson Skill 41a: Memory

Objective: To recall data necessary to answer story questions

Materials: A storybook

Procedure: Read a story aloud and ask each child questions about it. Start with questions about characters in the story. Then ask questions about the sequence and plot (which take more maturity to answer). Record the response level. (May be done during "Story.")

- Handwork: "All About Me" Book [Book completed in Daily Lesson Plans 4 - 7.]

Page 5: "Favorite Foods"

Materials: 8 1/2 x 11" paper, glue, magazine pictures of food

Procedure: Have each child choose pictures of favorite foods to glue onto his/her paper. Ask for the name of the food and then print it under each picture; also write "My Favorite Foods" at the bottom of the page.

Page 6: "Animals I Have or Like"

Materials: 8 1/2 x 11" paper, glue, magazine pictures of animals. Procedure: Have each child choose pictures of pets or favorite animals and glue them onto his/her paper. Ask for the name of each animal and then print it under each picture; also write "Animals I Have or Like" at the bottom of the page.

- Clean Up

- Pre-Story Activities: Weather, Days of Week, Songs, Fingerplays, Sharing Time

Special Activity C: "Alphabet Train"—Letter "B"

- Story

- Dismiss Group Procedure: Dismiss children by clothing color. Say, for example, "If you are wearing something green, you may go to the snack table."

- Snack

- Science Experience

- Outside Activities and/or Games

- Discuss Activities of the Day

- Prepare to Leave / Dismissal

Daily Lesson Plans

DAILY LESSON PLAN 7

Theme: Self-Awareness

- Free Play

Special Activity A: "Alphabet Book" — Letter "C" [See Table of Contents.]

Special Activity B: "All About Me" Book

Page 10: "My Shoe"

Materials: 8 1/2" x 11" paper, crayons

Procedure: Have each child remove a shoe. Place an 8 1/2 x 11" sheet of paper over the bottom of each shoe and rub crayon on the paper. This will reveal the shape and pattern of the shoe prints. Write "My Shoe Print" at the bottom of each page.

Lesson Skill 1: Language Development

Objective: To construct sentences using present tense verbs

Materials: Pocket chart, chalk, chalkboard, pictures (cut out from magazines) depicting individual people (family members) — adults, teenagers, children and babies (Be sure that all races are represented.)

Procedure: Display the pictures of people on the pocket chart. Discuss people as members of families and the activities that each family member does: cooking, mowing the lawn, washing the car, vacuuming, sewing, drawing pictures, playing ball, reading, typing. One by one, have each child point to a picture of a person and explain his/her role as a family member. Also, using a present tense verb, have each child tell about an activity done by his/her chosen person. Write each child's name and his/her sentence (containing the present tense verb) on the chalkboard. When all of the children's sentences have been recorded, read each one aloud, emphasizing its present tense verb.

Lesson Skill 87a: Visual Motor Coordination

Objective: To develop eye-hand coordination by writing name

Materials: Paper, pencil

Procedure: Have each child write as much of his or her own name as possible. Date and place these papers in the individual file folders. (Always encourage the children to write their names on their daily projects.)

- Handwork: "All About Me" Book [See DLP 4-7.]

Page 7: "My Family"

Materials: Magazine pictures of family members: adults, teenagers, children and babies, glue, 8 1/2 x 11" paper

Procedure: Each child chooses pictures to represent his/her family members and glues the pictures onto a sheet of paper. Write the name of the family member below each picture; also, the words "My Family" at the bottom of the page.

Page 8: "Things I Like to Do"

Materials: 8 1/2 x 11" paper, markers

Procedure: Discuss with the class members the things they enjoy doing or with which they like to play. To stimulate their thinking, ask them about what they like to play or do in their own yards, in their bedrooms and playrooms, on the playground and in school. Have the children draw pictures of their favorite things to play or do. While they are drawing, ask each child, in turn, to tell about his/her picture. Write their responses on their papers. Also, write "Things I Like to Do" at the bottoms of their pages.

- Clean Up

- Pre-Story Activities: Weather, Days of Week, Songs, Fingerplays, Sharing Time

Special Activity C: "Alphabet Train" — Letter "C"

- Story

- Dismiss Group Procedure: Dismiss the children one by one as they recognize their names written upon paper autumn leaves. For those who can't read, say the names aloud.

- Snack

- Science Experience

- Outside Activities and/or Games

- Discuss Activities of the Day

- Prepare to Leave / Dismissal

DAILY LESSON PLAN 8

Theme: Fall

- Free Play

Special Activity A: "Alphabet Book" — Letter "D"

Lesson Skill 16: Language Development

Objective: To increase vocabulary by naming fall objects

Materials: Fall objects such as: autumn leaves, a rake, an apple, an apple basket, an acorn, some Indian corn, a corn stalk, a football, a pumpkin

Procedure: Place all fall objects on a table. Have the children meet for a group time. Tell them that all of these objects have something to do with fall. Ask each child in turn to point out and identify an object on the table by saying, "This is a/an _____."

Lesson Skill 34a: Language Development

Objective: To enhance correct word pronunciation by saying initial sounds clearly [See Table of Contents.]

Materials: Initial Sound Cards, Pocket Chart

Procedure: Working with each child individually, have him/her select an initial sound card, identify the picture on it and place the card on the pocket chart. (Some children may make correct responses other than the desired one. If so, agree and then use the desired response in a sentence saying, "It is also _____. Say that for me.") Note and record any mispronounced sounds.

- Handwork: Four Seasons Picture Dial

Materials: 6" diameter construction paper circles, copies of the "Four Seasons" picture (circular shaped), glue, cardboard arrow pointed at one end, hole punched at other end, paper fastener, crayons

Procedure: Before class — write "Find the Fall Picture" to the left of the circle on the construction paper sheets.

During class — name and explain the seasons to the children. Then have each child glue a "Four Seasons" circle picture inside the larger circle drawn on the construction paper. Next, help the child to find the center point marked on his/her circle. Then insert a fastener through the arrow hole and the circles.

When all the children have completed the project, have them bring their Season Dials with them for a group time. Discuss the seasons of the year represented in the pictures. Have everyone find the fall picture and turn his/her dial to it.

- Clean Up

- Pre-Story Activities: Weather, Days of Week, Songs, Fingerplays, Sharing Time

Special Activity B: "Alphabet Train" — Letter "D"

- Story

- Dismiss Group Procedure: Dismiss the children one by one as they recognize their ages written on fall-colored leaves. Say the number on each leaf.

- Snack

- Science Experience

- Outside Activities and/or Games

- Discuss Activities of the Day

- Prepare to Leave / Dismissal

Daily Lesson Plans 19

DAILY LESSON PLAN 9

Theme: Fall

- Free Play

Special Activity A: "Alphabet Book"—Letter "E" [See Table of Contents.]

Lesson Skill 65: Visual Discrimination

Objective: To increase visual perception by classifying size, shape, and color

Materials: 3 sets of leaves, consisting of: 15 oak leaves (same color)—5 large, 5 medium, 5 small; 15 leaves (same colors)—5 maple, 5 oak; 15 maple leaves (three colors)—5 red, 5 yellow, 5 green.

Procedure: Working with each child individually, have him/her:

1) classify sizes by dividing the oak leaves into small medium and large sized piles;

2) classify shapes by dividing the maple, elm and oak leaves into similarly shaped piles;

3) classify colors by dividing the maple leaves into separate red, yellow and green piles.

Lesson Skill 85a: Visual-Motor Coordination

Objective: To develop eye-hand coordination by connecting dots on angular and curved lines

Materials: Prepared Lesson Sheets, pencils, crayons

Procedure: Have the children connect the dots from the leaves to the basket, in order to show where Jenni puts the leaves. Then have them color their pictures.

- Handwork: Leaf Preservation

Materials: Leaves, wax paper, plain white paper, iron, ironing board or thick cloth

Procedure: Have each child place his/her choice of leaves between two pieces of wax paper on an ironing board or a thick cloth. As the child watches, place the leaves and wax paper between two sheets of plain white paper (to protect the iron). Then iron the "leaves and paper sandwich" with a warm iron until the wax paper bonds together.

- Clean Up

- Pre-Story Activities: Weather, Days of Week, Songs, Fingerplays, Sharing Time

Special Activity B: "Alphabet Train"—Letter "E"

- Story

- Dismiss Group Procedure: Dismiss the children one by one as they recognize the initials of their first names written on paper autumn leaves.

- Snack

- Science Experience

- Outside Activities and/or Games

- Discuss Activities of the Day

- Prepare to Leave / Dismissal

DAILY LESSON PLAN 10

Theme: Fall

- Free Play

<u>Special Activity A</u>: "Alphabet Book" – Letter F
[See Table of Contents.]

Lesson Skill 49: Math Readiness

Objective: To establish a basis for understanding math by sorting objects on a grid

Materials: Tagboard grids (9" x 9") divided into 9 squares (each square 3" x 3"), construction paper to make 3 (yellow) leaves 3 (red) leaves and 3 (orange) leaves

Procedure: Working with each child individually, give him/her a grid, plus 3 yellow leaves, 3 red leaves and 3 orange leaves. Have each child arrange all the leaves on the grid in groups by color. (Do not try to correct the child if the pieces are not grouped appropriately.) Simply note and record his/her organizational development level.)

Lesson Skill 40a: Memory

Objective: To recall data necessary to repeat a series of numbers and a series of words

Procedure: Working with each child individually, have him/her listen to and repeat numbers. Start with 1/2 second intervals, building to 2 seconds between numbers. Start with a sequence of 2 numbers. When this is mastered, go on to a sequence of 3. Keep adding one more number to find out how many each child is able to recall. Give at least three examples for each sequence. Do the same with words. Include some fall words such as "pumpkin," "rakes," "apples," "football," "autumn leaves," and others.

- Handwork: Screen Painting

Materials: Leaves, 6"x 6" screens with masking tape around the edges, white paper, fall colored paints, paint brushes, paint shirts

Procedure: Have the children put a leaf or leaves under the screen on paper. Then holding the screen over the leaves, apply paint carefully so that the leaves do not move. Then lift the screen off the paper and discard the leaves.

- Clean Up

- Pre-Story Activities: Weather, Days of Week, Songs, Fingerplays, Sharing Time

<u>Special Activity B</u>: Matching Leaves

Procedure: Use the yellow leaves, red leaves, and orange leaves (from LS 49). Place one of each color on a separate row on the pocket chart. Have each child individually select a leaf from a bag, name its color, and place it on the pocket chart with the leaf of the same color.

<u>Special Activity C</u>: "Alphabet Train" – Letter "F"

- Story

- Dismiss Group Procedure: Dismiss the children one by one as they recognize their names written on leaves. Say the names aloud for those children who can not read them.

- Snack

- Science Experience

- Outside Activities and/or Games

- Discuss Activities of the Day

- Prepare to Leave / Dismissal

Daily Lesson Plans

DAILY LESSON PLAN 11

Theme: Fall

- Free Play

Special Activity A: "Alphabet Book" – Letter "G" [See Table of Contents.]

Lesson Skill 23: Language Development

Objective: To learn directional terms: up, down and around

Materials: A (completed) owl (see art project)

Procedure: Working with the children in small groups, tell the first child to move the owl up in the air, down to the floor and around the group. Then have him/her give the owl to a second child. Have the first child direct the second child to follow the same activity. Continue until all of the children have had a turn saying and acting out the three directions.

Lesson Skill 79a: Gross Motor Coordination

Objective: To improve large muscle abilities by using alternate feet to walk down steps

Materials: Steps

Procedure: Work with the children in small groups. Show them how to alternate their feet while walking down steps. Encourage each child to do this. Note and record their coordination.

- Handwork: Owl

Materials: Owls and wings drawn on white paper, scissors, crayons, brads

Procedure: Have the children color and cut out the owl and wings. Fasten the wings behind the body of the owl with a brad through the "x". Flap the owl's wings by moving them up and down.

- Pre-Story Activities: Pledge, Weather, Days of Week, Songs, Fingerplays, Sharing Time

Special Activity B: Fall Tree

Materials: A tree (without leaves) cut from brown felt, a felt board, leaves cut from red, yellow, orange, and green felt, (scale their size for placement on the tree), a cube (a large alphabet block or a cardboard box) with a leaf (red, yellow, orange, or green) glued onto each side

Procedure: Place the felt tree on the felt board. Have a child roll the cube. When it stops rolling, have him/her name the color of the leaf on the top side of the block. Then have him/her select a felt leaf to match the one on top of the cube and place the leaf on the tree.

Special Activity C: "Alphabet Train" – Letter "G"

- Story

- Dismiss Group Procedure: Draw a large owl on the chalkboard. Dismiss the children as they recognize their ages as you say them and write them on the owl.

- Snack

- Science Experience

- Outside Activities and/or Games

- Discuss Activities of the Day

- Prepare to Leave / Dismissal

DAILY LESSON PLAN 12

Theme: Fall

- Free Play

Special Activity A: "Alphabet Book"—Letter "M" [See Table of Contents.]

Lesson Skill 59: Visual Discrimination

Objective: To perceive and express relations of similarity and size

Materials: Apples of various sizes

Procedure: Work with children individually or in small groups.

Similarities—Show two apples to the children. Ask if the apples are the same or different. Vary the apple examples and ask again. Continue until all of the children give correct answers (and know the concept).

Size Comparisons—Show three apples: small-, medium- and large-sized to the children. Ask each of them to point out the large-sized apple, then the small-sized apple, and then the medium-sized apple. Then randomly point to the apples and have each of the children tell its size. Next, show the children two combinations of apples to exemplify each of the following size comparison concepts: taller/shorter, (two vertical rows) longer/shorter (two horizontal rows) and bigger/smaller. Then name one of the size comparison concepts and have the children point out a combination that exemplifies the concept. Next, point to each of the other combinations and have the children say the appropriate size comparison for each.

Lesson Skill 80a: Gross Motor Coordination

Objective: To improve large muscle abilities by walking backwards, walking on a balance board, and standing on each foot

Materials: A balance board

Procedure: Working with each child individually, show him/her how to walk backwards for six steps, to walk forwards on a balance board and to stand on each foot for five seconds. Note and record the coordination level of each child.

- **Handwork: Apple Basket Game**

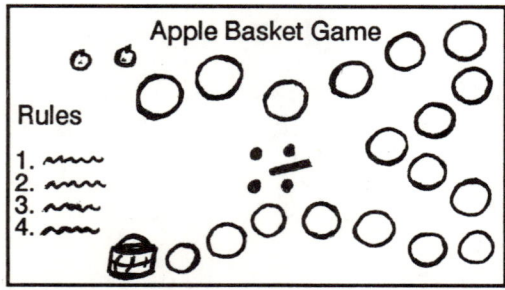

Materials: A game board of cardboard (8 1/2 x 11"), 1" circles of green, red, blue, and yellow, a cardboard spinner, a brad, some apple-shaped markers cut from red, green, yellow, and blue construction paper

Procedure: Name each of the colors in turn. Have the children glue circles of those colors on the dots on the game board. Help the children to attach the brads (spinners). (When finished playing, clip the apple markers to the game board to avoid loss.) Explain the rules (and write them on the back of the board):

1) Take turns starting.

2) Spin the dial.

3) Move the apple marker to the next circle along the path that is the same color as that to which the spinner pointed.

4) To win, be the first one to reach the last circle and place an apple on the basket.

- **Pre-Story Activities: Weather, Days of Week, Songs, Fingerplays, Sharing Time**

Special Activity B: "Alphabet Train"—Letter "H"

- **Story**

- **Dismiss Group Procedure:** Write the children's names in orange finger paint on individual papers. Dismiss the children one by one as they recognize their names as you show them. Read names for children who do not recognize them.

- **Snack**

- **Science Experience**

- **Outside Activities and/or Games**

- **Discuss Activities of the Day**

- **Prepare to Leave / Dismissal**

Daily Lesson Plans

DAILY LESSON PLAN 13

Theme: Fall

- Free Play

<u>Special Activity A</u>: "Alphabet Book" – Letter "I"
[See Table of Contents.]

Lesson Skill 29: Language Development

Objective: To increase listening comprehension through locating the source of hidden sounds

Materials: Music Box

Procedure: Have all of the children except one leave the room. He/she places a music box where it will be heard but not seen. The rest of the children return to the room and try to locate the music box by listening for where its sound is coming from. When the music box is found, all of the children except for the finder leave the room again. He/she then hides the music box in a new hiding place. Continue until all have had a chance to find the music box. (Instruct those who found it once not to tell where it is a second time, to give all a chance to find and hide it.)

Lesson Skill 83a: Fine Motor Coordination

Objective: To improve small muscle abilities by cutting on straight and curved lines.

Materials: Fall pictures cut from magazines (with pre-drawn puzzle cutting lines drawn on back with thick marker), scissors

Procedure: Instruct the children to choose a picture and make a puzzle out of it by cutting on the pre-drawn straight and curved lines. Be sure to give left-handed scissors to left-handed children.

- Hand Work: Pumpkin Man

Materials: Orange pumpkins and black hats drawn on construction paper, orange strips cut for legs and arms, scissors, glue and black crayons

Procedure: Have the children cut out their pumpkins and hats. Then have them draw in the facial parts with black crayon. Next, fold the arms and leg strips like accordions and glue them onto the pumpkins.

<u>Special Activity B</u>: "Alphabet Train" – Letter "I"

- Story

- Dismiss Group Procedure: Dismiss the children by the colors they are wearing.

- Snack

- Science Experience

- Outside Activities and/or Games

- Discuss Activities of the Day

- Prepare to Leave / Dismissal

DAILY LESSON PLAN 14

Theme: Fall

- Free Play

Special Activity A: "Alphabet Book" — Letter "J" [See Table of Contents.]

Lesson Skill 35: Language Development

Objective: To enhance correct word pronunciation by identifying words that rhyme

Materials: Pocket Chart, Rhyming Word Cards [See Table of Contents.]

Procedure: Working with each child individually, have him/her draw two cards from a pile and place them on the pocket chart. Next, ask the child to name the objects on both cards. Repeat the two named words and ask if they rhyme. Continue until every child understands the concept of rhyming words. Use some word sets that rhyme and some that do not.

Lesson Skill 81a: Fine Motor Coordination

Objective: To improve small muscle abilities by buttoning and tying

Materials: Shirts with buttons (larger buttons for younger children), shoes with laces

Procedure: Work with the children in small groups. Show them how to put a button through a button hole. Then have each child try it. Continue with tying knots and tying bows. Encourage the children to try these skills. However, if they are not ready, do not push.

- Handwork: Stuffed Turkey

Materials: Turkeys cut from large grocery bags (two for each child), crayons, staples, newspapers

Procedure: Staple the two turkeys together, leaving an opening for the newspaper stuffing. Have the children color their turkeys. Then wad up newspaper pages for turkey stuffing. Stuff, then staple the openings closed.

- Clean Up

- Pre-Story Activities: Weather, Days of Week, Songs, Fingerplays, Sharing Time

Special Activity B: Harvest Time / Thanksgiving

Procedure: Display a large turkey drawing on a wall. Discuss harvest celebrations and Thanksgiving. Ask each child to name something that he/she is thankful for (or likes or appreciates). Write each response on the large turkey. Then have the children write their names (or as much of them as they can) near their written responses.

Special Activity C: "Alphabet Train" — Letter "J"

- Story

- Dismiss Group Procedure: Dismiss the children one by one as they recognize their ages written on a turkey.

- Snack

- Science Experience

- Outside Activities and/or Games

- Discuss Activities of the Day

- Prepare to Leave / Dismissal

DAILY LESSON PLAN 15

Theme: Fall

- Free Play

Special Activity A: "Alphabet Book" — Letter "K" [See Table of Contents.]

Lesson Skill 73: Visual Discrimination

Objective: To increase visual perception by finding the path on a maze

Materials: Maze Lesson Sheet, crayons

Procedure: Discuss canoes and Native Americans. Instruct the children to draw a line on the shortest path from the Native American to the canoe on the maze.

Lesson Skill 82a: Fine Motor Coordination

Objective: To improve small muscle abilities by zipping and snapping clothing

Materials: A jacket with a good, working zipper, a jacket with snaps (jackets in adult and child sizes)

Procedure: Work with the children in small groups. Show them how to zip and unzip a jacket while wearing it. Warn them about catching fabric in the zipper's teeth. Then have them practice zipping and unzipping. Continue with a demonstration of snapping. Have the children practice snapping/unsnapping. Encourage them to try these skills. However, if they are not ready, do not push them.

- Handwork: Feather Headdress

Materials: Corrugated cardboard headbands (21" x 2 1/2"), feathers real or cut from various colors of construction paper, glue, felt markers, staples

Procedure: Have the children use felt markers to draw designs on the headbands. Then have them glue the feather tips into the corrugated "channels" of the cardboard. Next, fit the headbands around the children's heads and fasten the ends together with staples.

- Clean Up

- Pre-Story Activities: Weather, Days of Week, Songs, Fingerplays, Sharing Time

Special Activity B: "Alphabet Train" — Letter "K"

- Story: (During the story, have the children wear their headdresses and sit cross legged — like Indians — around a pretend campfire.)

- Dismiss Group Procedure: Place different-colored feathers, one at a time, on the felt board. Dismiss the children who are wearing clothes (other than their headdresses) that are the same color as the feather on the felt board.

- Snack

- Science Experience

- Outside Activities and/or Games

- Discuss Activities of the Day

- Prepare to Leave / Dismissal

DAILY LESSON PLAN 16

Theme: Fall

- **Free Play**

Special Activity A: "Alphabet Book" — Letter "L"
[See Table of Contents.]

Lesson Skill 67: Visual Discrimination

Objective: To increase visual perception by recognizing the whole picture from a partial view

Materials: Fall activity pictures (from magazines and calendars), cover pages with progressively sized sections cut out (to be positioned over a picture, so as to reveal only a portion of it at a time)

Procedure: Working with each child individually, ask if he/she can recognize the subject of the whole picture, even though he/she can only see part of it. If not, put a different cover page over the picture. Keep changing cover pages, if necessary, until the picture is completely revealed. Continue in the same manner with the remaining pictures.

Lesson Skill 84a: Fine Motor Coordination

Objective: To improve small muscle abilities by putting picture puzzles together

Materials: Picture Puzzles

Procedure: Have a group of four to six children work on individual puzzles. As each child finishes putting a puzzle together, count its pieces with him/her. Replace that puzzle with one having more pieces. Continue increasing the puzzles' difficulty until the child has trouble assembling it. Then help him/her to complete it. Note and record the number of pieces in the last puzzle completed independently.

- **Handwork: Fall Hikers (or Leaf Rakers)**

Materials: Fall hikers (pre-drawn on sheet), 1" x 6" tagboard strips (for supports), scissors, crayons, tape

Procedure: Have the children cut out the hikers and color them. Curve the supports into semicircles and tape them to the backs of the Hikers at boot level.

- **Clean Up**

- **Pre-Story Activities: Weather, Days of Week, Songs, Fingerplays, Sharing Time**

Special Activity B: Fall Activities

Procedure: Discuss the pictures of fall activities. Use prepackaged ones from publishers, calendars, study prints or those used in Lesson Skill 67. Ask the children what the people are wearing and what they are doing and why.

Special Activity C: "Alphabet Train" — Letter "L"

- **Story**

- **Dismiss Group Procedure:** Dismiss the children as they recognize the initial of their first names written on a turkey.

- **Snack**

- **Science Experience**

- **Outside Activities and/or Games**

- **Discuss Activities of the Day**

- **Prepare to Leave / Dismissal**

Daily Lesson Plans 27

DAILY LESSON PLAN 17

Theme: Fall

- Free Play

Special Activity A: "Alphabet Book" — Letter "M" [See Table of Contents.]

Lesson Skill 6: Language Development

Objective: To construct sentences using "yes" and "no" questions

Materials: List of questions requiring "yes" or "no" answers

Procedure: Work with the children in small groups. Ask them "yes" or "no" questions. Then have them ask questions about the same subjects. Examples of questions and leading statements are:

1) Did early people eat potato chips? Ask me if they ate some other kind of food.

2) Did early people wear snowmobile suits? Ask me if they wore some other clothing.

3) Did early people have electricity? Ask me if they used something else for light and heat.

4) Did early people live in log cabins? Ask me if they lived in some other type of home.

5) Did early people travel across the sea in campers? Ask me if they traveled in something else.

(Continue by discussing foods, clothing, homes, transportation, etc., as subjects for their questions.)

Lesson Skill 47a: Memory

Objective: To recall data necessary to name the days of the week

Procedure: Working with each child individually, ask him/her to say the days of the week. Record the responses in terms of the order in which they are given and completeness of the list.

- Handwork: Turkey

Materials: Drawings of turkeys, feathers from a feather duster, glue, crayons

Procedure: The children color their turkeys and then glue feathers on it.

- Clean Up

- Pre-Story Activities: Weather, Days of Week, Songs, Fingerplays, Sharing Time

Special Activity B: Thankful Book

Procedure: Explain that everyone will help to make a book entitled "We Are Thankful for People." Give each child a sheet of paper on which to draw a picture of a person they like and are thankful for. Upon completion, write "(child's name) is thankful for ___." on each paper. Collect all of the papers and staple them together to make a book. Read the book to the class and keep it in a place where the children may look at it in their free time.

Special Activity C: "Alphabet Train" — Letter "M"

- Story

- Dismiss Group Procedure: Place felt turkey on the felt board. One by one, add feathers of different colors to the turkey. Dismiss the children who are wearing the same color as the feathers.

- Snack

- Science Experience

- Outside Activities and/or Games

- Discuss Activities of the Day

- Prepare to Leave / Dismissal

DAILY LESSON PLAN 18

Theme: Explorers

- Free Play

Special Activity A: "Alphabet Book" — Letter "N"
[See Table of Contents.]

Lesson Skill 63: Visual Discrimination

Objective: To perceive and express the relationship of the quantities: more and less

Materials: Large lake cut from blue felt or flannel, six white felt boats, six red felt boats, felt board

Procedure: Working with the children in small groups, identify and then place the lake on the felt board. Place more white than red boats on the lake. Ask one child, "Are there more red boats, or more white boats?" Change the number of boats and ask another child which color boats there are more of. Continue until all of the children have identified "more" boats. Repeat, featuring comparisons using "less."

- Lesson Skill 39a: Memory

Objective: To recall the data necessary for following directions

Procedure: Give three activity directions to each child in turn. Have the him/her perform each of the assigned activities in their given sequence. Examples:

1) Close the door.
2) Get a drink from the drinking fountain.
3) Say "Hi!" to Mary.

1) Put a block in the block box.
2) Write something on the chalkboard.
3) Sit in a chair for a little while.

1) Put a piece on the felt board.
2) Ring the bell.
3) Give the goldfish some food.

1) Pound with the hammer.
2) Roll the ball.
3) Knock on the door.

The directions can be changed to provide many different sets of three. Modify the directions each time so that the children cannot imitate what someone else has done. Record the number of directions that each child follows.

- Handwork: Canoe Paddles

Materials: One paddle for each child (about 2' long cut from heavy cardboard), paint, paint brushes.

Procedure: Have the children paint their paddles. When the paddles are dry, have the children find positions, separate from each other, then kneel and pretend that they are paddling a canoe across the water.

- Clean Up

- Pre-Story Activities: Weather, Days of Week, Songs, Fingerplays, Sharing Time

Special Activity B: Explorers

Procedure: Talk about an explorer (Columbus, DeSoto, Ericsson, Champlain, Ride). Discuss the explorer's feats, the time when they occurred and the importance of his/her accomplishment.

Special Activity C: "Alphabet Train" — Letter "N"

- Story

- Dismiss Group Procedure: Dismiss the children one after another as they recognize their names written on small paper boats. Say the names aloud for those unable to read.

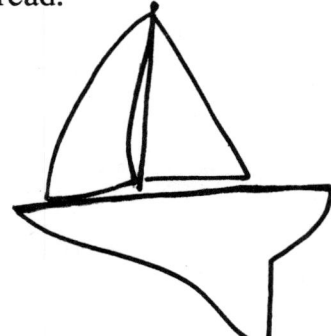

- Snack

- Science Experience

- Outside Activities and/or Games

- Discuss Activities of the Day

- Prepare to Leave / Dismissal

Daily Lesson Plans

DAILY LESSON PLAN 19

Theme: Shapes (Circles and Ovals)

- Free Play

Special Activity A: "Alphabet Book"—Letter "O" [See Table of Contents.]

Lesson Skill 76: Visual Discrimination

Objective: To increase visual perception by matching shapes and letters

Materials: Lesson Sheets, pencils

Procedure: Instruct the children to circle the shape or letter in each row that matches the first one shown.

Lesson Skill 55a: Math Readiness

Objective: To establish a basis for understanding math by naming numbers

Procedure: Ask each child, individually, to count as high as possible.

- Handwork: Oval Juggler

Materials: Oval juggler drawn on sheet, several 1" paper circles (precut), crayons, glue (The number of circles should equal the number of letters in each child's name.)

Procedure: Have each child glue circles, (one for each letter in his/her first name) in pre-marked spots, in an arc above the juggler's head. Next, have the child write the letters of his/her name on the circles, one letter on each. Then have the children draw faces on and color their jugglers.

- Clean Up

- Pre-Story Activities: Weather, Days of Week, Songs, Fingerplays, Sharing Time

Special Activity B: Shape Land Castle

Materials: Large drawing of Shape Land Castle, assortment of shapes—squares, rectangles, circles, triangles, diamonds.

Procedure: Have children draw circles and other shapes in the air. Explain and name the shapes. Then place a drawing of Shape Land Castle on the bulletin board. One at a time, have the children choose a shape (from squares, rectangles, circles or triangles), tell what it is, and then find one like it on the Shape Land Castle. Staple the shape onto the castle.

Special Activity C: "Alphabet Train"—Letter "O"

- Story

- Dismiss Group Procedure: Dismiss the children as they recognize their names written on circles. Say the names aloud for those children who are unable to read them.

- Snack

- Science Experience

- Outside Activities and/or Games

Procedure: Place a string on the ground in the shape of an oval. Have the children name all the things they can think of that are like the shape made by the string.

- Discuss Activities of the Day

- Prepare to Leave / Dismissal

DAILY LESSON PLAN 20

Theme: Shapes (Squares and Rectangles)

• Free Play

Special Activity A: "Alphabet Book" — Letter "P"
[See Table of Contents]

Lesson Skill 64: Visual Discrimination

Objective: To increase visual perception by copying patterns

Materials: Rectangular shaped oak tag cards marked with square grids and square shaped pieces of construction paper (to fit into the grid spaces)

Procedure: Place the squares of construction paper in various pattern arrangements on a tagboard card. Have the children copy the same patterns on their cards.

Lesson Skill 56a: Math Readiness

Objective: To establish a basis for understanding math by counting objects

Materials: Square pieces of construction paper mounted along a wall or placed on a table top

Procedure: Working with each child individually, instruct him/her to count as many of the squares as possible. Have the child touch the squares as he/she says each number. (Be sure the children work from left to right to aid correct eye-hand coordination.)

• Handwork: Robot

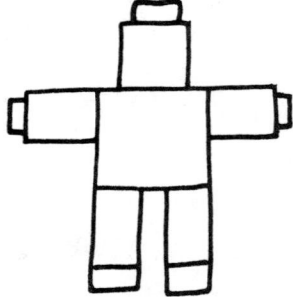

Materials: Multiple copies of robot drawing, construction paper squares and rectangles to fit onto squares and rectangles drawn on the robot, glue

Procedure: Talk about the rectangle and square shapes of construction paper. Show the children the robot and talk about the shapes that are drawn on the robot. Give each child a robot page, and some squares and rectangles. Have the children cover the squares and rectangles on the robot with the corresponding construction paper pieces and glue them in place. Finally, have the children draw faces on their robots.

• Clean Up

• Pre-Story Activities: Weather, Days of Week, Songs, Fingerplays, Sharing Time

Special Activity B: Square Shapes

Procedure: Have the children stand in lines to form the sides of a square and then join hands. Repeat to form a rectangle.

Special Activity C: "Magic Shape Wands"

Materials: 12" x 1" lengths of heavy cardboard (one for each child), construction paper shapes: rectangles, squares, triangles, and circles

Procedure: (Glue a shape to the end of each cardboard strip.) Have each child choose a wand and identify its shape. Then have him/her find the same shape on the Shape Land Castle. Also, have him/her find — 1) the same shape that is the same size, 2) the same shape that is larger, and 3) the same shape that is smaller than the shape on his/her wand.

Special Activity D: "Alphabet Train" — Letter "P"

• Story

• Dismiss Group Procedure: Point out letters of the alphabet written on a large square. Dismiss the children one by one as he/she recognizes his/her own first initial among the letters.

• Snack

• Science Experience

• Outside Activities and/or Games

Procedure: Have children use stones to make lines to form the sides of squares and rectangles.

• Discuss Activities of the Day

• Prepare to Leave / Dismissal

Daily Lesson Plans

DAILY LESSON PLAN 21

Theme: Shapes (Triangles and Diamonds)

- Free Play

<u>Special Activity A</u>: "Alphabet Book" — Letter "Q" [See Table of Contents.]

Lesson Skill 72: Visual Discrimination

Objective: To increase visual perception by reproducing triangle patterns

Materials: Triangle design forms (drawn on paper), construction paper triangles (cut to fit into the triangle spaces), envelopes

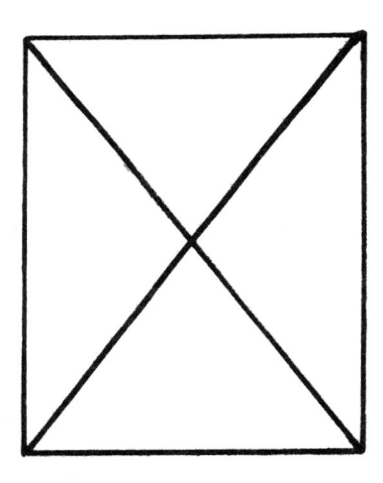

Procedure: Working with the children in small groups, give each child a triangle design form and some triangles. Arrange triangle pieces in designs on a triangle design form. Have the children duplicate the designs on their forms. Also, have the children make designs of their own. Then have the children put their triangles into envelopes to take home.

Lesson Skill 89a: Visual-Motor Coordination

Objective: To develop eye-hand coordination by using left-to-right and top-to-bottom progression

Materials: Two Lesson Sheets for each child — one for left-to-right progression, the other for top-to-bottom progression, pencils

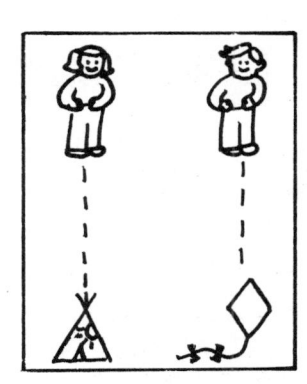

Procedure: Give each child a left-to-right progression lesson sheet. Explain that Danny and Jenni are each walking toward different road signs. Ask the children to draw lines on the dots that connect Danny and Jenni to their respective road signs. Next, give each child the lesson sheet for top-to-bottom progression. Explain that Jenni and Danny are each walking toward different toys. Have the children draw lines on the dots that connect Jenni and Danny to the toys. Also, talk about the shapes of the toys.

- **Handwork: Triangle/Diamond Forms**

Materials: Two Design Form Lesson Sheets featuring triangle and diamond shapes for each child, crayons, scissors, envelopes

Procedure: Have the children color and cut out the shapes on one design form lesson sheet. Discuss the features of the shapes. Then have the children match their cutout shapes to the shapes on the second design form lesson sheet. Finally, have the children put the shapes in envelopes to take home.

- Clean Up

- Pre-Story Activities: Weather, Days of Week, Songs, Fingerplays, Sharing Time

Special Activity B: Air Triangles and Diamonds

> Procedure: Draw triangle and diamond shapes in the air. Have the children imitate the movements to produce the shapes.

Special Activity C: Locating Shapes

> Procedure: Have each child choose a "magic shape wand" (see "Special Activity" in DLP 12) and identify the shape on its end. Hold a yardstick across the "Shape Land Castle" on the bulletin board. Ask each child to point to a shape on the castle, above or below the yardstick, that matches the shape on his/her wand.

Special Activity D: "Alphabet Train" — Letter "Q"

- Story

- Dismiss Group Procedure: Place triangles and diamond shapes, one for each child, in a bag. Have each child pick out a shape from the bag and identify it. Tell the children that those with triangles may go to the snack table. Then those with diamonds may go.

- Snack

- Science Experience

- Outside Activities and/or Games

> Procedure: Tie the ends of a 9' length of string together. Then have three children form three points of a triangle while holding onto the string. Add one more child (a fourth point) and have them form a diamond shape. Have enough strings and groups of children to insure participation by every child.

- Discuss Activities of the Day

- Prepare to Leave / Dismissal

DAILY LESSON PLAN 22

Theme: Shapes (Circles, Ovals, Squares, Rectangles, Triangles, Diamonds)

- Free Play

Special Activity A: "Alphabet Book" — Letter "R" [See Table of Contents.]

Lesson Skill 60: Math Readiness

Objective: To perceive and express relationships of placement (first, middle, last) and distance (near, far)

Materials: 3 triangles (10" on each side)

Procedure: Have each child, one at a time, stand in front of three triangles placed in a row (at 12" intervals) on the floor. Ask the child to stand on the first triangle, then on the middle triangle and then on the last triangle. The order may be changed. Then have the child return to the front of the triangles. Ask him/her to stand on the triangle that is most near and then the triangle that is most far. (The order may be changed.)

Lesson Skill 86a: Visual Motor Coordination

Objective: To develop eye-hand coordination by copying a square, a circle and a triangle

Materials: Paper, pencil

Procedure: Working with each child individually, draw a square on the paper. Ask him/her to draw a second square on this paper. Continue in the same manner with circles and triangles. Date these papers and place them in the children's individual file folders.

- **Handwork: Shapes Matching Game**

Materials: Shape boxes (3 for each child, made from eight ounce milk cartons and covered with plain paper), red, green, and blue construction paper to make: 7 circles (3 red, 2 green, 2 blue), 7 squares (2 red, 3 green, 2 blue), and 7 triangles (2 red, 2 green, 3 blue), glue

Procedure: (Cut the tops off all of the milk cartons and wrap them with paper.) Have each child glue a red circle on one box, a green square on another box and a blue triangle on another. Then have the children put the other shapes into their boxes, matching them according to shape and/or color.

- Clean Up

- Pre-Story Activities: Weather, Days of Week, Songs, Fingerplays, Sharing Time

Special Activity B: Air Shapes

Procedure: Draw shapes (circles, ovals, squares, rectangles, triangles, diamonds) in the air.

Special Activity C: "Magic Shape Wand"

Procedure: Have each child choose a "magic shape wand" (see Special Activity C in DLP 12), and then point out the same shape on the "ShapeLand Castle" with his/her wand.

Special Activity D: "Alphabet Train" — Letter "R"

- Story

- Dismiss Group Procedure: Dismiss the children one by one as they recognize the initials of their first names written on a large sheet of paper cut in the shape of a circle.

- Snack

- Science Experience

- Outside Activities and/or Games

Procedure: Paint shapes on concrete with water.

- Discuss Activities of the Day

- Prepare to Leave / Dismissal

DAILY LESSON PLAN 23

Theme: Winter Holidays

- Free Play

Special Activity A: "Alphabet Book" — Letter "S"
[See Table of Contents.]

Lesson Skill 54: Math Readiness

Objective: To establish a basis for understanding math by remembering order of objects

Materials: A tube (10" long x 3" in diameter), 3 pieces of cardboard (one gift-wrapped in blue paper, one in red, and one in yellow), a yard long length of yarn

Procedure: (Use the yarn to tie each of the 3 pieces of cardboard together in a sequence: first the blue, then the red, then the yellow.) Working with each child individually, explain that each of the wrapped cardboards is a gift package. Then ask him/her to name the colors of each of the gifts. (If he/she is unable to do so, have a duplicate set of wrapped gifts ready for the child to point to, instead of having to name the colors.) To administer the test, slowly draw the gifts through the tube, asking the child to name (or point to) the color of each gift as it enters that tube. When the gifts are all in the tube, ask the child to name (or point to) the color of the gift that will come out first. Then pull the first gift out of the tube to reveal its color. Continue in the same manner with the second and third gifts. This test may be repeated with the gifts in the same order or in the reverse order. Note and record the ability level of the individual children.

Lesson Skill 43b: Memory

Objective: To recall data necessary to name body parts

Materials: Mirror, paper, pencil

Procedure: Work with the children individually. Have each child name as many of his/her body parts as possible. For clarity and reinforcement, try using a large mirror in which both teacher and child can point out and see the various parts. Record the date and the body parts that each child names. File the list in the child's individual file folder (for another progress comparison later in the year).

- Handwork: Candle Holder (can be Menorah or other)

Materials: Wood pieces (soft wood such as pine or balsa) 1" x 2" x 9", a 1/4" drill, clamps, white birthday candles

Procedure: (Before class — Mark 8 dots, 1" apart, on several pieces of wood.) Clamp a piece of wood to the tabletop. Demonstrate how to drill holes into each of the dots. Next, have each child drill a hole. Give him/her as much help as needed. Finally, have each child place a candle in the hole that he/she drilled.

- Clean Up

- Pre-Story Activities: Weather, Days of Week, Songs, Fingerplays, Sharing Time

Special Activity B: The Menorah

Procedure: Talk about the importance of light, its uses, its varieties, its symbolism. Discuss what night would be like without lights.

Special Activity C: "Alphabet Train" — Letter "S"

- Story

- Dismiss Group Procedure: Dismiss the children as they recognize the initials of their first names written on construction paper gifts.

- Snack

- Science Experience

- Outside Activities and/or Games

- Discuss Activities of the Day

- Prepare to Leave / Dismissal

Daily Lesson Plans

DAILY LESSON PLAN 24

Theme: Winter

- Free Play

Special Activity A: "Alphabet Book" — Letter "T" [See Table of Contents.]

Lesson Skill 53: Math Readiness

Objective: To obtain a basis for understanding math by recalling an absent object

Materials: 8" x 8" tagboard cards showing a grid of 4 squares (each square 4" x 4"), 4 different cookie cutters

Procedure: Working with each child individually, have him/her place one cookie cutter on each square. Ask him/her to turn around while you remove one cutter and place it out of sight. Then the child looks at the grid and tells which cookie cutter is missing. Continue this procedure a few more times. Then reverse roles. Have the child remove a cookie cutter while you are not looking; then tell which one is missing.

Lesson Skill 77b: Gross Motor Coordination

Objective: To improve large muscle abilities by running, skipping, jumping, hopping

Procedure: Have each child run, skip, jump and hop from a designated point. Note and record his/her coordination. (May be done during "Outside Activity" time.)

- **Handwork: Window shade Pulls (or Tree Ornaments)**

Materials: Cookie cutters, glitter (variety of colors), wire (for hangers), a rolling pin, cornstarch clay (Recipe: Mix, stir and boil 2 cups salt and 2/3 cups water. Add 1 cup cornstarch and 1/2 cup cold water. Stir on burner until thick. Mix just before using.)

Procedure: (Make cornstarch clay. Cover its container to keep it supple.) Give each child a portion of clay. Help him/her to roll the clay flat. Then have him/her use the cookie cutters to cut out window shade pulls. Next, sprinkle the pulls with glitter. Also, attach a wire hanger. Let the pulls dry for a day or two before allowing the children to take them home.

- Clean Up

- Pre-Story Activities: Weather, Days of Week, Songs, Fingerplays, Sharing Time

Special Activity B: Calendar Tree

Procedure: Hang a large cutout of a fir tree on a wall. Display the days of the month on it. Use pictures of snowflakes to cover each day of the week as it passes.

Special Activity C: "Alphabet Train" — Letter "T"

- Story

- Dismiss Group Procedure: Dismiss the children as they recognize the words, (seemingly) said by a puppet, that start with the same sounds as the children's first names.

- Snack

- Science Experience

- Outside Activities and/or Games

- Discuss Activities of the Day

- Prepare to Leave / Dismissal

DAILY LESSON PLAN 25

Theme: Winter

- Free Play

Special Activity A: "Alphabet Book" — Letter "U"
[See Table of Contents.]

Lesson Skill 12: Language Development

Objective: To construct sentences using adjectives

Materials: Objects or pictures of winter sports equipment and clothing

Procedure: Working with each child individually, present one object or picture at a time. Ask, "What is this?" After the correct identification is made, have each child tell something about the size, color or shape of the item. Help the child to use descriptive adjectives in his/her sentences ("This is a big, red bow.") Continue this procedure with several objects.

Lesson Skill 88b: Visual Motor Coordination

Objective: To improve eye-hand coordination by drawing a person

Materials: Chalkboard, chalk, paper, crayons

Procedure: Draw a picture of a person on the chalkboard as the children suggest body parts. Then have each child draw a picture of a person on paper. Write each child's name and the date on his/her paper and file it in the child's individual file folder.

- Handwork: Child-Sized Fir Tree

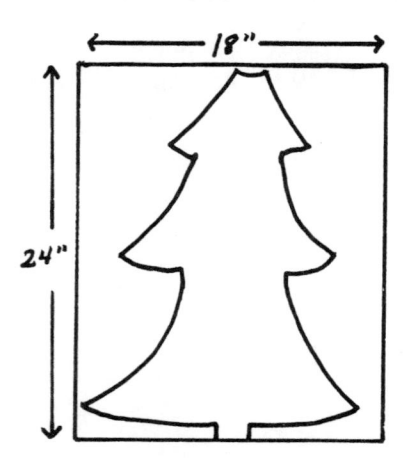

Materials: Fir trees cut from green construction paper, brown pine cones and white snowflakes drawn on construction paper, scissors, glue, masking tape, 18" lengths of string (for ties)

Procedure: (Make fir trees for all of the children. Punch holes near the left and right tips of the top tree branches. Reinforce the holes.) Give each child a tree and some pine cones and snowflakes to cut out and then glue onto the tree. Next, attach ties to the reinforced holes. Then help the children to hang their trees around their necks. Make sure the ties are not too tight. (With all of the children disguised as a forest of trees, this is a good time to take a photograph.)

- Clean Up

- Pre-Story Activities: Weather, Days of Week, Songs, Fingerplays, Sharing Time

Special Activity B: "Alphabet Train" — Letter "U"

- Story

- Dismiss Group Procedure: Dismiss the children as they hear a puppet (seemingly) say words that rhyme with their names.

- Snack

- Science Experience

- Outside Activities and/or Games

- Discuss Activities of the Day

- Prepare to Leave / Dismissal

DAILY LESSON PLAN 26

Theme: Winter

- Free Play

<u>Special Activity A</u>: "Alphabet Book" — Letter "V" [See Table of Contents.]

Lesson Skill 38: Language Development

Objective: To enhance correct word pronunciation by identifying words with same initial sound as the child's name

Materials: A bell, a list of words that start with the same sounds as the children's names

Procedure: Working with each child individually, have him/her say the initial sound in his/her name. Then say a list of words, some with the same initial sound and others without it. Have the child ring the bell when he/she hears a word that has the same initial sound as his/her name. Then have the child say the word and his/her name, emphasizing the beginning sound.

Lesson Skill 78b: Gross Motor Coordination

Objective: To improve large muscle abilities by throwing and catching a ball

Materials: A ball, 8" or larger

Procedure: From a distance of 4 to 8 feet, have each child throw the ball to the teacher and then catch it. Repeat the exchange several times to determine the child's level of skill and to have fun. Record the level for the child's individual file. Compare with earlier performance. (May be done during "Outside" time.)

- **Handwork: Winter Holiday Figures of Your Choice**

Materials: Winter theme figures (skaters, sledders) drawn on white paper, scissors, crayons

Procedure: Have the children color and cut out the figures. (Then have them fold on the fold lines, or add braces to make the figures stand up.)

- Clean Up

- Pre-Story Activities: Weather, Days of Week, Songs, Fingerplays, Sharing Time

<u>Special Activity B</u>: Winter Sports

Procedure: Show a picture of winter sports and have the children name objects in it.

<u>Special Activity C</u>: "Alphabet Train" — Letter "V"

- Story

- Dismiss Group Procedure: Dismiss the children as they recognize their ages written on fir trees.

- Snack

- Science Experience

- Outside Activities and/or Games

- Discuss Activities of the Day

- Prepare to Leave / Dismissal

DAILY LESSON PLAN 27

Theme: Winter

- Free Play

<u>Special Activity A</u>: "Alphabet Book" — Letter "W" [See Table of Contents.]

Lesson Skill 26: Language Development

Objective: To learn directional terms — top, bottom, sides, open, close

Materials: A styrofoam snowball, a box with a cover into which the snowball will fit

Procedure: Work with each child individually. Tell him/her to:

1) Put the snowball on the top of the box.
2) Put the snowball by the side of the box.
3) Open the box.
4) Put the snowball on the bottom of the box.
5) Close the box.

Next, repeat all of the steps (1 - 5) and have the children tell each step. (Questions such as "What did I do?" or "Where is the snowball?" may be needed to get the children to use the correct directional words.)

Lesson Skill 42b: Memory

Objective: To recall data necessary to name colors

Materials: Color Wheel

Procedure: Working with each child individually, have him/her name the colors pointed to on the Color Wheel. Note and record the unfamiliar colors. Help the child to learn one or two new colors in reference to colored objects in the room.

- Handwork: Wreath

Materials: Wreaths and bows cut from construction paper, soap flakes, water, green food coloring, round red cinamon candies

Procedure: Mix a small amount of water with the soap flakes to make a thick mixture. Add green food coloring to the mixture. Have the children spread the soap flake mixture all over their wreaths. To finish, have them decorate their wreaths with a bow and cinnamon candies.

- Clean Up

- Pre-Story Activities: Weather, Days of Week, Songs, Fingerplays, Sharing Time

<u>Special Activity B</u>: Gifts

Procedure: Talk about giving and receiving gifts. Have a small present, such as a sucker, gift wrapped for each child. Ask the children why people give presents to others. Give them their wrapped gifts. Ask them: "What is on the outside?", "How do you feel when someone gives you a gift?" and "How can you find out what is inside?" Have them open the gifts. Ask them, "What do you tell someone who gives you a gift?" and "How do they feel when you say, "thank you?".

<u>Special Activity C</u>: "Alphabet Train" — Letter "W"

- Story

- Dismiss Group Procedure: Dismiss the children as they recognize their names written on a snowman. Read names aloud for children who do not recognize them.

- Snack

- Science Experience

- Outside Activities and/or Games

- Discuss Activities of the Day

- Prepare to Leave / Dismissal

Daily Lesson Plans

DAILY LESSON PLAN 28

Theme: Winter

- Free Play

Special Activity A: "Alphabet Book"—Letter "X" [See Table of Contents.]

Lesson Skill 66: Visual Discrimination

Objective: To increase visual perception by completing a picture

Materials: Lesson Sheet, pencils, crayons, cotton, glue

Procedure: Instruct the children to draw lines to complete the boot's outline. Then have them glue cotton on top of the boots and color them.

Lesson Skill 41b: Memory

Objective: To recall data necessary to answer story questions

Materials: A storybook

Procedure: Read a story aloud and ask each child questions about it. Start with questions about characters and then go on to sequence and plot. Record the response level. (This may be done during Story.)

- Handwork: Greeting Cards for Parents

Materials: Red construction paper with candle cut-outs on the front (8 1/2" x 11") folded in half (at the 5 1/2" midpoint), foil sheets (8 1/2" x 5 1/2"), glue, markers, white paper sheets (3 1/2" x 4 1/2") for personalized inscriptions

Procedure: Have the children glue pieces of foil inside their cards (to cover the cutout candles). Next, have them glue the white inscription papers onto the insides (right) of their cards. Then write the children's dictated messages as they watch. Have the children sign the cards themseves. They may also draw pictures.

- Clean Up

- Pre-Story Activities: Weather, Days of Week, Songs, Fingerplays, Sharing Time

Special Activity B: Winter Visitor

Procedure: Make arrangements to have someone with a winter-related occupation (snowplow operator, ski patrol person, ice sculptor) come to school. Prepare children for this visit by having them think of questions that they want to ask the visitor about his/her occupation. Tape record their conversations with the visitor for them to hear later.

Special Activity C: "Alphabet Train"—Letter "X"

- Story

- Dismiss Group Procedure: Dismiss the children as they recognize the initials of their first names written on a picture of a snow boot.

- Snack

- Science Experience

- Outside Activities and/or Games

- Discuss Activities of the Day

- Prepare to Leave / Dismissal

DAILY LESSON PLAN 29

Theme: Winter

- Free Play

Special Activity A: "Alphabet Book" — Letter "Y"
[See Table of Contents.]

Lesson Skill 17: Language Development

Objective: To increase vocabulary by naming winter items

Materials: Mittens, gloves, scarves, hats, snowsuits, jackets, snow pants, books, ice, snow, sleds, toboggans, skis, skates, etc.

Procedure: Have the children gather together for a group time. Tell them that all the objects on the table are associated with winter. Then, have each child, in turn, pick up an object from the table and say, "This is a/an ____."

Lesson Skill 87b: Visual-Motor Coordination

Objective: To develop eye-hand coordination by writing name

Materials: Paper, pencil

Procedure: Have each child write as much of his/her name as possible. Date and place these papers in the individual file folders. (Encourage all of the children to write their names on their daily projects.)

- Handwork: Doily Snow Person

Materials: Three circular paper lace doilies for each child — one 6", one 5", and one 4", blue construction paper (11 1/2" x 18"), glue, construction paper cutouts for each child — noses, mouths, hats, eyes, buttons, brooms, and scarves, black crayon

Procedure: Have the children glue their 6" doilies near the bottom edges of their construction paper. Then have them glue the 5" doilies above the 6" ones (with a slight overlap). Next, have them glue the 4" doilies, (the snow people's heads) in place above the 5" ones (again, with a slight overlap). Have them use a black crayon to draw sticks (arms) on their snowpeople. To finish, have them glue the hats, eyes, noses, mouths, buttons, and brooms in place.

- Clean Up

- Pre-Story Activities: Weather, Days of Week, Songs, Fingerplays, Sharing Time

Special Activity B: Winter Pictures

Procedure: Make a collage of winter pictures cut from magazines. Have each child choose a picture to glue onto a large paper on a wall. Title the collage "Winter".

Special Activity C: "Alphabet Train" — Letter "Y"

- Story

- Dismiss Group Procedure: Dismiss the children as they hear the snow person puppet say words that rhyme with their names. (The words used do not need to be real words; they only have to rhyme with their names.)

- Snack

- Science Experience

- Outside Activities and/or Games

Special Activity D: Outside Clothes

Procedure: Label a bulletin board "I Am Learning to Dress Myself for Outside Play". On it place a cutout of a snowsuit or a jacket (in warmer climates) for each child. Write each child's name on a garment.

- Discuss Activities of the Day

- Prepare to Leave / Dismissal

Daily Lesson Plans 41

DAILY LESSON PLAN 30

Theme: Winter

- Free Play

Special Activity A: "Alphabet Book" — Letter "Z"
[See Table of Contents.]

Lesson Skill 52: Math Readiness

Objective: To establish a basis for understanding math by matching objects of proportionate size

Materials: 3 Socks — small, medium, and large; 3 boots — small, medium, and large (cut from paper)

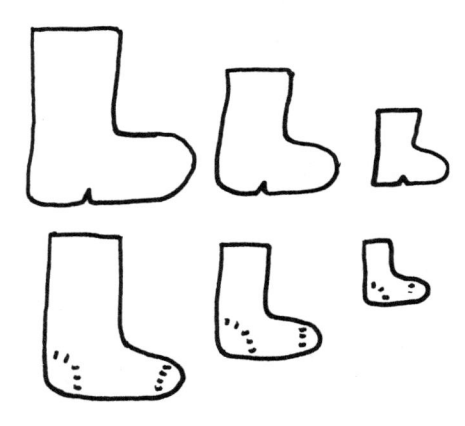

Procedure: Working with each child individually, place the socks and boots on a table. Have the child make the best fits of boot to sock (large to large, medium to medium, small to small). Note and record his/her level of perceptual development.

Lesson Skill 34b: Language Development

Objective: To enhance correct word pronunciation by saying initial sounds clearly

Materials: Initial Sound Cards, Pocket Chart

Procedure: Working with each child individually, have him/her pick up the cards, one at a time from the pile, say what the picture shows, and then place the cards on the pocket chart. (The child might not say the desired response. If so, agree with any correct word and say, "It is also _____. Say that for me." Note and record any mispronounced sounds.

- **Handwork: Book of Winter Clothing**

Materials: Construction paper (3" x 4") for front and back covers, 4 white sheets of paper (3" x 4") for each child, glue, staples, and magazine pictures showing jackets, snow pants, hats, boots, and mittens

Procedure: (Write "Outside Winter Clothing" on all of the front covers; also, staple the 4 white sheets of paper between the front and back covers.) Have each child glue a snowsuit or a jacket and snow pants onto page 1, a hat onto page 2, a pair of mittens onto page 3 and a pair of boots onto page 4.

- Clean Up

- Pre-Story Activities: Weather, Days of Week, Songs, Fingerplays, Sharing Time

Special Activity B: Tobogganing

Procedure: Place 2' x 6' long sheets of paper on the floor. (Have sheets enough to be sure that all of the children will have a place.) Have the front rider in each toboggan sit cross-legged, while the rest of the riders put their feet into the lap of the rider in front of him/her. Next, have each rider pretend that he/she is riding down a steep hill. Talk about the things they can imagine they are passing.

Special Activity B: Alphabet Train — "Z"

- Story

- Dismiss Group Procedure: Dismiss the children as they hear the snow person say words that start with the same sound as their names.

- Snack

- Science Experience

- Outside Activities and/or Games

- Discuss Activities of the Day

- Prepare to Leave / Dismissal

DAILY LESSON PLAN 31

Theme: Winter

- Free Play

<u>Special Activity A</u>: "Alphabet Book" — Compilation [See Table of Contents.]

Lesson Skill 44: Memory

Objective: To recall data necessary to sequence pictures

Materials: Story pictures (sequences)

Procedure: Working with each child individually, give him/her a set of story pictures, and then tell the following story to the child. "First there was no snow. Then it started to snow. Then there was lots of snow on the ground." Ask the child to retell the story using the story pictures.

Lesson Skill 85b: Visual Motor Coordination

Objective: To develop eye-hand coordination by connecting dots on angular and curved lines

Materials: Snowball Roll Lesson Sheet, pencils, crayons

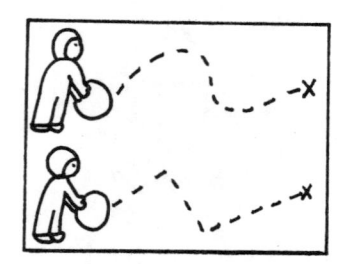

Procedure: Have the children connect the dots to show where Danny will roll a snowball. They may color their pictures.

- Handwork: Soapflake Winter Scene

Materials: Blue construction paper (11" x 18"), soap flakes mixed with water to make a thick paste

Procedure: Talk with the children about things that are outside and white in the wintertime — snowmen, igloos, clouds, snow-covered trees and house roofs. Have the children spread the soap flake mixture on the blue construction paper with their hands, making designs and/or pictures.

- Clean Up

- Pre-Story Activities: Weather, Days of Week, Songs, Fingerplays, Sharing Time

<u>Special Activity B</u>: "Alphabet Train" completion

Procedure: Have the children review the 26 letters on the train cars and name an object that starts with each letter. Explain that the "Alphabet Train" is now complete.

<u>Special Activity C</u>: Snow Person Pieces

Procedure: Have each child select and then place a part of a felt snow person on the felt board. Start with the base.

- Story

- Dismiss Group Procedure: Dismiss the children as they recognize the initials of their first names written on mittens. Have the children find and then hang their mittens with matching mittens on a clothesline hanging along a wall. Be sure to have duplicates of letters for the children with the same first initial.

- Snack

- Science Experience

- Outside Activities and/or Games

Procedure: Have the children draw with sticks in the snow.

- Discuss Activities of the Day

- Prepare to Leave / Dismissal

DAILY LESSON PLAN 32

Theme: Jobs

- Free Play

Lesson Skill 3: Language Development

Objective: To construct sentences using future tense verbs

Materials: Magazine pictures of people doing jobs, mounted on tagboard or heavy construction paper

Procedure: Work with each child individually (or in small groups). Ask the children to choose pictures of people at work, doing jobs that the children would like to do when they grow up. Have each child hold up a picture and say, "When I grow up, I will be a ____."

Lesson Skill 40b: Memory

Objective: To recall the data necessary to repeat a series of numbers and a series of words

Procedure: Working with each child individually, say a series of numbers and ask him/her to listen to and repeat the numbers. Start with 1/2 second intervals, building to 2 seconds between numbers. Start with a sequence of 2 numbers. When this is mastered, go on to a sequence of 3. Keep adding one more number to find out how many each child is able to recall. Give at least three examples for each sequence. Do the same with words. Include some words describing jobs: chef, mechanic, draftsman, acrobat, artist, model, writer, accountant, singer, actor, scientist, forester, banker, plumber, teacher, builder, pilot, nurse, doctor, carpenter, dentist, detective, custodian, mail carrier, farmer, dancer, fire fighter, police officer, veterinarian, miner, psychiatrist, tailor.

- Handwork: Child / Adult Pictures

Materials: Magazine pictures of adults in various occupations and of active children, glue, sheets of paper (8 1/2" x 11") with lines dividing them in half lengthwise

Procedure: On each paper write "Now I am a child learning many new things," on the left side, and "When I grow up, I will be a _____." on the right side. Have each child first choose a picture of a child that resembles himself/herself, and then a picture of an adult working at a job that the child would like to have when he/she is an adult. Next, have the child glue the picture of the child on the left side of the line and the picture of the adult on the right side.

- Clean Up

- Pre-Story Activities: Weather, Days of Week, Songs, Fingerplays, Sharing Time

Special Activity B: Jobs

Procedure: Invite several parents to come in and tell what their jobs are and where they work. Have them show the tools and/or equipment they use and the clothes that they wear. Have the children act out these job roles.

Special Activity C: Green

Procedure: Show the color green. Have the children name green objects. Have them find things in the room that are green.

- Story

- Dismiss Group Procedure: Make color cards by cutting construction paper or felt rectangles and mounting them on 8 1/2" x 5 1/2 tagboard cards. Include green, blue, gray, orange, yellow, brown, white, black, red, pink and purple. Write the name of the color on its card. To increase their durability, cover the cards with clear contact film. Show the color cards, identifying each color. Dismiss the children one by one as each recognizes the colors on their clothing.

- Snack

- Science Experience

- Outside Activities and/or Games

- Discuss Activities of the Day

- Prepare to Leave / Dismissal

DAILY LESSON PLAN 33

Theme: Jobs

- Free Play

Special Activity A: "Book of Colors" / Blue

Special Activity B: Personal Dimensions

Procedure: Measure and record the children's heights on height chart. Also, record the date and children's weights on their anecdotal record sheets.

Lesson Skill 28: Language Development

Objective: To increase listening comprehension by solving riddles (Who am I? What is it?)

Materials: Magazine pictures or drawings of career workers and the clothing they use

Procedure: Work with children in small groups. Have one child choose a picture of a career worker. He/she says, "Who am I?" and acts out and talks about what the worker does. When the children have guessed the job, another child chooses another picture and acts out and talks about that worker's job. Continue until all children have had a turn. Next, use this "acting/talking" method to present "What is it?" questions by having the children act out and talk about using the clothing, tools, or equipment in the picture. Have each child take a turn saying, "What is it?"; then acting out and talking about "its" use.

Lesson Skill 80b: Gross Motor Coordination

Objective: To improve large muscle abilities by walking backwards, walking on a balance board, and standing on each foot

Materials: Balance board

Procedure: Working with each child individually, show him/her how to walk backwards six steps, how to walk forward, and how to stand on each foot for five seconds on a balance board. Note and record the coordination level of each child.

- Handwork: Chef's Apron

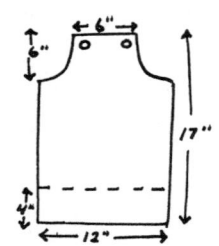

Materials: Aprons cut out of brown paper bags, large paper bag rectangles (pockets for the aprons) a stapler, a hole punch, hole reinforcements, yarn (for ties), cooking utensils drawn on construction paper, scissors

Procedure: Fold pocket up on fold line. Then staple along its side edges. Punch two holes where indicated on the illustration. Reinforce the holes and tie one end of a length of yarn to the left hole and the other end of the yarn to the right hole. Have the children cut out the cooking utensils and put them in their apron pocket.

- Clean Up

- Pre-Story Activities: Weather, Days of Week, Songs, Fingerplays, Sharing Time

Special Activity C: More Jobs

Procedure: Invite more parents to come in and tell what their jobs are and where they work. Have them show the tools and/or equipment they use and the clothes that they wear. Have the children act out various job roles.

Special Activity D: Blue

Procedure: Show the color blue. Have the children name blue objects. Have them find things in the room that are blue.

- Story

- Dismiss Group Procedure: Show color cards and identify each color. Dismiss the children one by one as they recognize the colors on their clothing.

- Snack

- Science Experience

- Outside Activities and/or Games

- Discuss Activities of the Day

- Prepare to Leave / Dismissal

Daily Lesson Plans 45

DAILY LESSON PLAN 34

Theme: Peace

- **Free Play**

Special Activity A: "Book of Colors"—Gray

Lesson Skill 74: Visual Discrimination

 Objective: To increase visual perception by pairing things that go together

 Materials: Skill Lesson Sheet, crayons

 Procedure: Have the children draw lines from the workers to the tools/equipment used in their work. Also, have the children color the pictures.

Lesson Skill 79b: Gross Motor Coordination

 Objective: To improve large muscle abilities by alternating feet while walking down steps

 Materials: Steps

 Procedure: Work with the children in small groups. Show them how to alternate their feet while walking down steps. Note and record their levels of coordination.

- **Handwork: Peace Prize Medallions**

 Materials: Cardboard circles (4" diameter), gold or silver foil circles (8 1/2" diameter, to wrap cardboard circles), yarn, punch, drawing paper, permanent marker pens, hole reinforcers, paper circles (8" diameter)

 Procedure: (Wrap the cardboard circles—one for every child—with foil, then punch a hole at the top of each foil-covered circle. Next, use permanent marker to write "Peace Prize Medallion" on the disk.)

 Discuss the concept of peace with the children, pointing out the following:

 1) that when problems come up, they should be handled by discussing them and doing what is best for most people,

 2) that we cannot always have our own way, and

 3) that it is not a good idea to threaten or hurt others to make things go our own way.

 Also, talk about possible problems in the school room, on the playground, in stores and elsewhere, as well as with parents, brothers and sisters. Next, have the children think of something they can do to solve a problem peacefully. Have them draw pictures of their ideas on the circular paper. When the pictures are done, ask each child what his/her picture shows about peace, and write the response along the bottom of the picture. Then punch a hole near the top of the picture. Place a hole reinforcer on the hole center, thread a length of yarn through the hole and through the medallion in front. After tying a knot (to secure the medallion to the picture), tie the "Peace Prize Medallion Picture" around its creator's neck.

- **Clean Up**

- **Pre-Story Activities: Weather, Days of Week, Songs, Fingerplays, Sharing Time**

Special Activity B: Peace Pictures

 Procedure: Show and read the captions on the "Peace Prize Medallion" pictures.

Special Activity C: Famous Peacemakers

 Procedure: Tell the children about famous peacemakers. Tell who they were and what they accomplished in their lifetimes. Tell what troubles they had and what honors they received.

Special Activity D: Visitor

 Procedure: Invite a lawyer to visit the class. Ask him/her to tell the children about laws and about being a lawyer and working with people to solve their problems. Before hand, have the children make a list of questions to ask the visitor about his/her profession.

Special Activity E: Gray

 Procedure: Show the color gray. Have the children name objects that are gray. Have them find things in the room that are gray.

- Story

- Dismiss Group Procedure: Show color cards and identify each color. Dismiss the children one by one as they recognize the colors on their clothing.

- Snack

- Science Experience

- Outside Activities and/or Games

- Discuss Activities of the Day

- Prepare to Leave / Dismissal

Daily Lesson Plans

DAILY LESSON PLAN 35

Theme: Senses

- Free Play

Special Activity A: "Book of Colors" — Orange
[See Table of Contents.]

Lesson Skill 30: Language Development

Objective: To increase listening comprehension through exposure to environmental sounds

Materials: Tape recording of household sounds such as water running from a faucet, closing a door or noises from a typewriter, doorbell, piano, washing machine, blender, mixer, pencil sharpener, vacuum cleaner, telephone, timer, clock, alarm clock, and smoke alarm

Procedure: Work with the children in small groups. Have them listen to the tape of household sounds. Pause between each sound and have the children take turns guessing what the sounds are.

Lesson Skill 89b: Visual-Motor Coordination

Objective: To develop eye-hand coordination by using left-to-right progression and top-to-bottom progression

Materials: Two Lesson Sheets for each child, one for left-to-right progression and one for top-to-bottom progression, pencils

Procedure: Give the children lesson sheets for left-to-right progression. Tell them that Danny likes to see the sun and the moon. Have them draw lines from Danny to the sun and from Danny to the moon. Next, give the children lesson sheets for top-to-bottom progression. Tell them that Jenni hears the dog bark and the bell ring. Have them draw lines from Jenni to the dog and from Jenni to the bell.

- Handwork: Binoculars

Materials: 2 toilet tissue tubes for each child, masking tape, hole punch, yarn, felt markers

Procedure: Help the children to tape two tubes together. Then punch a hole on the outside of each tube and tie the end of a length of yarn into each hole (to make a strap for hanging the binoculars from around the neck). Have the children color their binoculars with felt markers.

- Clean Up

- Pre-Story Activities: Weather, Days of Week, Songs, Fingerplays, Sharing Time

Special Activity B: Flashlight Tag

Materials: 2 flashlights

Procedure: Have two children at a time shine flashlight spots, with one trying to catch the other's spot on the ceiling, walls or floor. Continue until all of the children have had a turn.

- Story

- Dismiss Group Procedure: Show color cards and identify each color. Dismiss the children one by one as they recognize the colors on their clothing.

- Snack

- Science Experience

- Outside Activities and/or Games

Special Activity C: Surfaces

Procedure: Have the children feel various objects with their elbows, knees, foreheads, arms or legs. (Use rough, smooth, plush, and sticky surfaced objects.)

- Discuss Activities of the Day

- Prepare to Leave / Dismissal

DAILY LESSON PLAN 36

Theme: Senses

- Free Play

Special Activity A: "Book of Colors" — Yellow
[See Table of Contents.]

Lesson Skill 51: Math Readiness

Objective: To establish a basis for understanding math by matching objects by touch

Materials: Textured fabrics (two of each kind) mounted on cards; include velvet, fake furs, terry cloth, textured double knits, satin and others

Procedure: Place one card of each kind of fabric in a paper bag. Set the other matching cards on a table. Working with each child individually, have him/her reach into the bag, select a card, feel its fabric, and match it with one of the cards on the table.

Lesson Skill 86b: Visual-Motor Coordination

Objective: To develop eye-hand coordination by copying a square, a circle and a triangle

Materials: Paper, pencil

Procedure: Working with each child individually, first draw a square on the paper, and then ask the child to duplicate the drawing of the square. Continue with circles and triangles. Date the child's paper and place it in his/her individual file folder.

- Handwork: Hand Print Rubber Band Board

Materials: Boards (8" x 8" x 3/4"), 1 1/2" finishing nails, hammer(s), rubber bands, permanent markers

Procedure: Have each child place a hand on a board. With permanent markers, trace around each child's hand. Next, help the children to pound nails into the wood at the tops and bottoms of the finger outlines. Then have the children connect the nails with rubber bands.

- Clean Up

- Pre-Story Activities: Weather, Days of Week, Songs, Fingerplays, Sharing Time

Special Activity B: Face Slides

Procedure: Show slides of happy, sad, and mad faces. (To make these slides, clean unwanted slides using chlorine bleach and draw faces on with permanent felt markers.) As they view the slides, have the children tell how they think the people feel. Talk about why they may feel that way. Talk about facial parts (eyes and mouth) that express emotions.

Special Activity C: Yellow

Procedure: Show the color yellow. Have the children name objects that are yellow. Then have the children find things in the room that are yellow.

- Story

- Dismiss Group Procedure: Show color cards, identifying each color. Dismiss the children one by one as they recognize the colors on their clothing.

- Snack

- Science Experience

- Outside Activities and/or Games

Procedure: Listen for outside sounds with the children and tape record them. Play them inside the next time you meet; have the children identify the different sounds.

- Discuss Activities of the Day

- Prepare to Leave / Dismissal

DAILY LESSON PLAN 37

Theme: Family

- Free Play

Special Activity A: "Book of Colors" — Brown
[See Table of Contents.]

Lesson Skill 22: Language Development

Objective: To increase vocabulary by naming family members

Materials: Pictures of people to represent father, mother, sister, brother, grandfather and grandmother

Procedure: Have the children meet for a group time with the family members. The family members stand in front of the class and say which family member he or she is. Then have the children, one at a time, point to each family member as you say "father, mother, sister, brother, grandmother and grandfather" (order may be changed). Then have each child say who the family members are as you point to them.

Lesson Skill 39b: Memory

Objective: To recall data necessary to follow directions

Procedure: Give three directions or commands to each child.

Examples:

1) Talk on the telephone.	1) Stir some soup.
2) Drink some milk.	2) Shovel some snow.
3) Roll a ball.	3) Sweep the floor.
1) Eat a sandwich.	1) Dust the furniture.
2) Set the table.	2) Paint the wall.
3) Wash dishes.	3) Put toys in the toy box.

The directions can be changed to provide many different sets of three. Have the children act out the directed behaviors. Change the directions each time to avoid mere imitation of behavior. Note and record the number of directions that each child follows.

- Handwork: Family Story Spinner

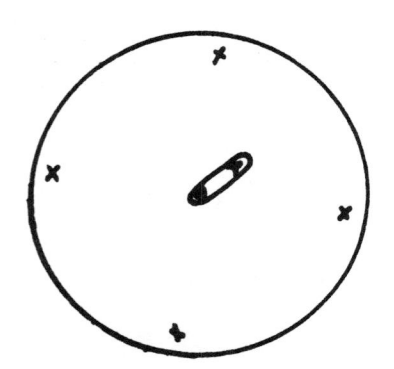

Materials: Magazine pictures of people (to represent all of the members of each child's immediate family), construction paper circles (8 1/2" in diameter), glue, large safety pins, paper fasteners, marker

Procedure: (Cut all of pictures into circles 2 1/2" in diameter.) Mark each child's large circle with x's (one for each family member). Then have the children glue their family member pictures onto the x's. Write the names of the family members below their pictures. Help the child to make a spinner by inserting a brad through the bottom end of a closed safety pin and into the center hole of the large circle. Explain that after they spin a spinner, the children should say something good about the person to whom the spinner is pointing.

- Clean Up

- Pre-Story Activities: Weather, Days of Week, Songs, Fingerplays, Sharing Time

Special Activity B: Family Story

Procedure: One at a time, have the children spin to an individual person on their "Family Story Spinners." Have each child tell to whom the spinner is pointing and also something good about that person.

Special Activity C: Brown

Procedure: Show the color brown and have the children name objects that are brown. Have the children find things in the room that are brown.

- Story

- Dismiss Group Procedure: Show color cards and identify each color. Dismiss the children one by one as they recognize the colors on their clothing.

- Snack

- Science Experience

- Outside Activities and/or Games

- Discuss Activities of the Day

- Prepare to Leave / Dismissal

DAILY LESSON PLAN 38

Theme: Address

- Free Play

Special Activity A: "Book of Colors" — White [See Table of Contents.]

Lesson Skill 4: Language Development

Objective: To construct sentences using "when" and/or "where" questions

Materials: Doll house and furniture for "when" questions

Procedure: For "when" questions, have the children meet as a group. Have each child choose a piece of furniture from the doll house. One by one, each child says to the child seated next to himself/herself, "This is a chair. When do you use it?" The next child answers. Then that child tells the next child "This is a ____. When do you use it?" That child answers and the activity continues until all of the children have had a turn to answer and ask a question.

For "where" questions, have the children sit in a circle. Start by saying to a child, "I live on ____ Street. Where do you live?" The child responds with his/her street and asks the next child where he or she lives. (Tell the children the names of their streets if the children do not know.)

Lesson Skill 55b: Math Readiness

Objective: To establish a basis for understanding math by naming numbers

Procedure: Ask each child, individually, to count as high as possible.

- Handwork: House

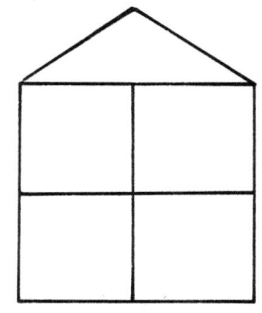

Materials: House-shaped paper or cardboard cutout (16" x 12"), magazine pictures of bedrooms, living rooms, kitchens and bathrooms (6" x 6" or less), glue

Procedure: (Draw lines dividing the house cutouts into 4 equal squares.) Have each child choose a picture of a bedroom, a living room, a kitchen and a bathroom. Then have him/her glue their picture choices into the squares.

- Clean Up

- Pre-Story Activities: Weather, Days of Week, Songs, Fingerplays, Sharing Time

Special Activity B: Rooms

Procedure: Have each child point to a room in the house he or she made during art time, tell what it is and name one object in that room.

Special Activity C: White

Procedure: Show the color white. Have the children name objects that are white and find things in the room that are white.

- Story

- Dismiss Group Procedure: Dismiss the children by address, showing each child's address on an individual envelope and saying "The address on this envelope is number __, ____ street, in _____ city." If a child does not recognize his/her address, say, "The name is _____."

- Snack

- Science Experience

- Outside Activities and/or Games

Special Activity D: Homes

Procedure: Have the children take a walk around the block. Have them notice the different kinds of places where people live, such as apartment buildings, mobile homes, houses, duplexes. Also, have them notice the different types of materials that homes are made of. If the weather or area does not permit the previous activity, talk about the above things and tell the children to notice different types of homes as they are traveling. Also, have them notice what materials their own homes are made of.

- Discuss Activities of the Day

- Prepare to Leave / Dismissal

DAILY LESSON PLAN 39

Theme: Telephone

- Free Play

<u>Special Activity A</u>: "Book of Colors" — Black

Lesson Skill 5: Language Development

Objective: To construct sentences using "what" and "who" questions

Materials: A bowl, the names of classroom jobs written on cards with drawings to illustrate what needs to be done in the classroom (Jobs may include sorting out misplaced objects, straightening out the book shelves, dusting furniture, sweeping floors, washing tables, caring for classroom animals, erasing chalkboards, cleaning paint brushes, etc.)

Procedure: Have the children meet as a group. Tell them that there are many jobs to be done and that these jobs are written on cards in the bowl. Next, ask, "Who will select a job card first?" Choose a volunteer to draw a card. Ask him/her, "What is the job?" After the child answers, have him/her keep the card and ask, "Who will draw the next job card?" Choose another child. After the second child has drawn a card, have the first child ask "What is the job?" Continue until all of the children have asked a "What" and a "Who" question. After all of the children have received a job card, have the children do the jobs.

Lesson Skill 56b: Math Readiness

Objective: To establish a basis for understanding math by counting objects

Materials: An abacus

Procedure: Move all beads on the abacus over to the left hand side. Have the children move one bead over to the right side as they say each number. (Be sure they work from left to right to aid eye-hand coordination.)

- **Handwork: Telephone Number Worm Puzzle**

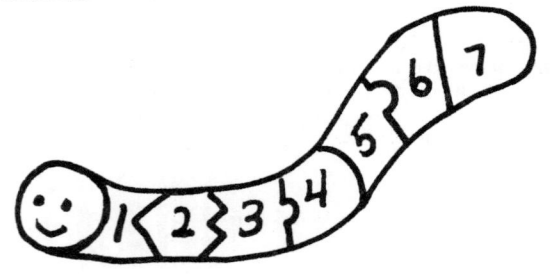

Materials: Worm puzzles drawn on heavy construction paper with each child's telephone number, scissors, envelopes

Procedure: The children cut out the pieces in their telephone number worm puzzles and put them together. Go over the telephone numbers with each child using the worm puzzle. Each child places his or her puzzle pieces in an envelope to take home.

- Clean Up

- Pre-Story Activities: Weather, Days of Week, Songs, Fingerplays, Sharing Time

<u>Special Activity B</u>: Gossip Game

Procedure: Have the children sit in a circle. Whisper a sentence, such as "The sky is blue.", to the first child to the right. That child whispers it to the next child to the right, and so on until the sentence goes all around the circle. The last child says the sentence out loud. Tell the children the original message and see how it compares. Continue this game by reversing directions (message to the left) and by having the children change their positions in the circle and starting another sentence.

- Story

- Dismiss Group Procedure: Show color cards and identify each color. Dismiss the children one by one as they recognize the colors on their clothing.

- Snack

- Science Experience

- Outside Activities and/or Games

<u>Special Activity C</u>: Telephone lines

Procedure: Observe the telephone lines outside. Discuss how voices are carried over the lines from one point to another.

- Discuss Activities of the Day

- Prepare to Leave / Dismissal

DAILY LESSON PLAN 40

Theme: Valentine's Day

- Free Play

<u>Special Activity A</u>: "Book of Colors" — Red
[See Table of Contents.]

Lesson Skill 10: Language Development

Objective: To construct sentences using pronouns

Materials: A heart cut from red construction paper

Procedure: Have the children meet as a group. Have one child pass the heart to another child and say, "I gave the heart to him/her." The child who received the heart says, "He/she gave this heart to me." Then the second child then gives the heart to another child, repeating what was said to him/her. Continue passing the heart and saying the sentences until all of the children have participated.

Lesson Skill 83b: Fine Motor Coordination

Objective: To improve small muscle abilities by cutting on straight and curved lines

Materials: Straight and curved lines drawn on red construction paper, scissors

Procedure: Instruct the children to cut on the straight lines and on the curved lines. (Be sure to give left-handed scissors to those children who need them.)

- Handwork: Valentines for Families

Materials: White construction paper (8 1/2" x 11"), large (3" across) red construction paper hearts, smaller (1" across) red construction paper hearts (enough for one heart for every person in each child's family and sized to fit on the front of each child's card), strips of white construction paper (1/2" x 5 1/2", accordion folded, one per child), glue

Procedure: (Fold the construction paper sheets in half. Write "Happy Valentine's Day" on the outside, front cover of each card and "My Heart Leaps for You" on the large heart.) Have each child glue a small heart (one for each person in his/her family) on the front of the card. Write a family member's name on each heart. Glue one end of the accordion folded strip on the inside (right page) of the card and glue the large heart onto the other end of the strip. Have each child write his/her name on his/her card. (Fold the accordion strips so the hearts will leap out when the card is opened.)

- Clean Up

- Pre-Story Activities: Weather, Days of Week, Songs, Fingerplays, Sharing Time

<u>Special Activities B</u>: Heart Felt

Procedure: Make heart-shaped puzzles from red felt. Have the children take turns putting pieces of the puzzles together on the felt board.

<u>Special Activities C</u>: Red

Procedure: Show the color red. Have the children name objects that are red. Then have them find things in the room that are red.

- Story

- Dismiss Group Procedure: Show color cards and identify each color. Then dismiss the children one by one as they recognize the named colors on their clothing.

- Snack

- Science Experience

- Outside Activities and/or Games

- Discuss Activities of the Day

- Prepare to Leave / Dismissal

DAILY LESSON PLAN 41

Theme: Valentine's Day

- Free Play

Special Activity A: "Book of Colors" — Pink
[See Table of Contents.]

Lesson Skill 25: Language Development

Objective: To learn the directional terms "in front of" and "in back of," as well as "inside," "on" and "between"

Materials: Valentine Puppet (see Handwork below), 2 boxes decorated for Valentine's Day

Procedure: Working with each child individually, have him/her hold the puppet in front of, in back of, inside, on and between the boxes. Then hold the puppet in these positions and have the child describe the placement of the puppet, using all of the above directional words.

Lesson Skill 81b: Fine Motor Coordination

Objective: To improve small muscle abilities by buttoning and tying

Materials: Shirts with buttons (larger buttons for younger children), shoes with laces

Procedure: Work with the children in small groups. Show them how to put a button through a button hole. Then have each child try to do it. Continue in the same manner with tying knots and tying bows. Encourage the children to try these skills. However, do not push if the children are not ready.

- **Handwork: Valentine Puppets**

Materials: 4 hearts — 1 large (3"), 1 medium (2"), and 2 small (1") — and 2 strips cut from heavy construction paper, glue, markers

Procedure: (Cut holes in the bottoms of the large hearts.) Have the children assemble and glue the 4 hearts and 2 paper strips. Then have them draw faces on their puppets. Finally, show them how to put their fingers through the holes (at the bottoms of the large hearts) to make their puppets walk.

- Clean Up

- Pre-Story Activities: Weather, Days of Week, Songs, Fingerplays, Sharing Time

Special Activity B: White

Procedure: Show the color white and have the children name objects that are white. Also, have them find things in the room that are white.

Special Activity C: Right

Procedure: Tape a red heart on each child's right shoe. Tell the children the heart is on their right shoes. Have them lift their right shoes. Talk about right legs, hands, arms, ears, eyes, etc., as well.

- Story

- Dismiss Group Procedure: Show the color cards and identify each color. Dismiss the children one by one as they recognize the colors on their clothing.

- Snack

- Science Experience

- Outside Activities and/or Games

- Discuss Activities of the Day

- Prepare to Leave / Dismissal

Daily Lesson Plans

DAILY LESSON PLAN 42

Theme: Valentine's Day

- Free Play

Special Activity A: "Book of Colors" — Purple
[See Table of Contents.]

Lesson Skill 36: Language Development

Objective: To enhance correct word pronunciation by identifying words with the same initial sound

Materials: Initial Sound Cards, Valentine's box with slot on top

Procedure: Work with each child individually. Show him/her three initial sound cards, two that start with the same sound and one that does not. Have the child name the items that are pictured on the cards. Emphasize the items' initial sounds. Encourage him/her to hear and recognize the first sound in each word and to determine which two words start with the same sound. After he/she chooses the correctly matching sounds (with help if necessary), have him/her put the cards in the Valentine's box.

Lesson Skill 82b: Fine Motor Coordination

Objective: To improve small muscle abilities by zipping and snapping clothing

Materials: Jacket with a good working zipper, jacket with snaps (jackets in adult and child sizes)

Procedure: Work with the children in small groups. Show them how to zip and unzip the jacket while wearing it. Then have them try. Continue in the same manner with snapping. Encourage the children to try these skills. Do not push if they are not ready.

- **Handwork: Valentine People**

Materials: Six hearts drawn on red construction paper (a large one for the body, a medium-sized one for the head, four small ones for the feet), four hearts cut from white construction paper for eyes, nose and mouth, and four white construction paper strips (1/2" x 4") for arms and legs, glue and scissors

Procedure: Have the children cut out the hearts and accordion fold the white strips. Then have each child glue the white strips and the red hearts together (to make a Valentine Person). Next, glue the white hearts (eyes, nose, and mouth) onto the red heart head.

- Clean Up

- Pre-Story Activities: Weather, Days of Week, Songs, Fingerplays, Sharing Time

Special Activity B: Purple

Procedure: Show the color purple. Have the children name objects in the room that are purple.

Special Activity C: Colored Hearts

Procedure: Cut out and draw faces on hearts of all colors (happy, sad, mad). Have each child choose a heart. Have him/her tell the color of the heart, imitate the expression on the heart and tell if the face is happy, sad or mad.

- Story

- Dismiss Group Procedure: Show color cards and identify each color. Dismiss the children one by one as he or she recognizes the color on his/her clothing.

- Snack

- Science Experience

- Outside Activities and/or Games

- Discuss Activities of the Day

- Prepare to Leave / Dismissal

DAILY LESSON PLAN 43

Theme: Patriotic Holidays

- Free Play

Special Activity A: "Book of Colors" — Compilation [See Table of Contents.]

Lesson Skill 37: Language Development

Objective: To enhance correct word pronunciation by identifying words that rhyme with one's name

Procedure: Work with the children in groups of two or three. Start by saying each child's name and a word that rhymes with it. Then have each child say the two rhyming words together and talk about the fact that they rhyme. Repeat this procedure with each child a few times. Then say words that may or may not rhyme with the child's name. If so, have the child raise his/her hand and say the word and his/her name together. (The words used do not have to be real words; they need only to rhyme with the children's names.)

Lesson Skill 84b: Fine Motor Coordination

Objective: To improve small muscle abilities by putting puzzles together

Materials: Puzzles

Procedure: Have four to six children working simultaneously on individual puzzles. As each child finishes a puzzle, count the pieces with him/her. Replace that puzzle with one having more pieces. Continue increasing the puzzles' difficulty until the child has trouble assembling one. Then help him/her to complete it. Note and record the number of pieces in the last puzzle completed independently.

- Handwork: The National Flag

Materials: A line drawing of the national flag on white paper, crayons (in the colors of the flag), paper stars/stripes/national symbols (as appropriate for flag).

Procedure: Have the children color the flags in national colors, then stick on the stars/stripes or symbols. (Discuss what the colors and symbols on the flag represent to the citizens of the nation.)

- Pre-Story Activities: Weather, Days of Week, Songs, Fingerplays, Sharing Time

Special Activity B: Famous People

Procedure: Show pictures of famous patriots or other people whose works have benefited people. Talk about the differences and similarities in their looks. Talk about the ways in which clothing and hair styles differ in various historic times. Compare some with the styles of today.

Special Activity C: Money Pictures

Procedure: Show patriots' and political figures' pictures on coins and pieces of paper currency. Then discuss why these people are shown on money.

- Story

- Dismiss Group Procedure: Dismiss the children as they recognize words that rhyme with their names.

- Snack

- Science Experience

- Outside Activities and/or Games

- Discuss Activities of the Day

- Prepare to Leave / Dismissal

DAILY LESSON PLAN 44

Theme: Transportation

- Free Play

Special Activity A: "Numeral Book of Tiny Things" — "One" [See Table of Contents.]

Lesson Skill 2: Language Development

Objective: To construct sentences using past tense verbs

Materials: Blocks, toy car

Procedure: Have the children help set up a village made of blocks. Then have each child carefully "drive" a toy car wherever he/she wants in the village (as long as the buildings are left standing). Next, ask each child to retrace his/her route verbally. Help the children to form sentences containing past tense verbs (to tell where they drove).

Lesson Skill 47b: Memory

Objective: To recall data necessary to name the days of the week

Procedure: Working with each child individually, ask him/her to name the days of the week. Record the responses in terms of the order in which they are given and completeness of the list.

- Handwork: Travel Bag

Materials: Construction paper (8 1/2" x 11"), staples, paper punch, yarn, glue, lesson sheet showing pictures of items needed for overnight travel, pictures of transportation modes

Procedure: Have the children fold the 8 1/2" x 11" papers in half (matching bottom to top). Then staple along the right and left edges. Next, punch holes in the top right and top left corners and tie yarn from one hole to the other (to form a handle). Write "Travel Bag" on the side of each bag. Next, have the children cut out the overnight travel items. Discuss the items and have the children place them in their travel bags. Finally, have them select and glue transportation pictures on the outside of their bags.

- Clean Up

- Pre-Story Activities: Weather, Days of Week, Songs, Fingerplays, Sharing Time

Special Activity B: Travel Bag

Procedure: Have a small suitcase (or some type of travel bag) packed with items children would need for overnight travel. Showing the items one by one, have the children name each item. (Items may include pajamas, toothbrush, toothpaste, soap, towel, washcloth, comb, brush, and teddy bear.) Also, have the children discuss places where they would like to stay overnight.

- Story

- Dismiss Group Procedure: (Write each child's address on a paper mailbox.) Show and read the mailbox addresses, one by one. Dismiss the children as they recognize their addresses.

- Snack

- Science Experience

- Outside Activities and/or Games

- Discuss Activities of the Day

- Prepare to Leave / Dismissal

DAILY LESSON PLAN 45

Theme: Transportation

- Free Play

Special Activity A: "Numeral Book of Tiny Things"— "Two" [See Table of Contents.]

Lesson Skill 62: Visual Discrimination

Objective: To perceive and express relationships of speed (fast, slow)

Procedure: Working with the children in groups of two, accompany the children as they walk, jump, and swing their legs, fast and slow. Then tell one of the children to do one of these activities. He/she may do it fast or slow. Have another child tell whether the activity is being done fast or slow. Continue until all of the children have done the activities and determined whether they were done fast or slow.

Lesson Skill 77c: Gross Motor Coordination

Objective: To improve large muscle abilities by running, skipping, jumping, hopping

Procedure: Have each child run, skip, jump and hop to the Teacher from a designated point. Note and record his/her coordination. (May be done during "Outside" time.)

- Handwork: Bus

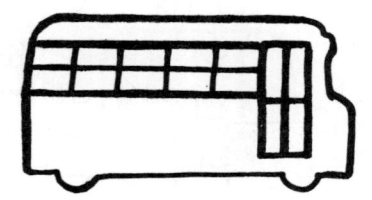

Materials: A bus drawn on heavy paper, scissors, felt markers

Procedure: Have the children draw pictures of friends and family riding on the bus. Write the names of the people under their pictures.

- Clean Up

- Pre-Story Activities: Weather, Days of Week, Songs, Fingerplays, Sharing Time

Special Activity B: Transportation

Procedure: Talk about all the different kinds of ways that the children could come to school: bus, car, truck, walk, bike or train; let the children use their imaginations.

- Story

- Dismiss Group Procedure: Dismiss the children as they recognize their names written on paper cars. Read names for children who do not recognize them.

- Snack

- Science Experience

- Outside Activities and/or Games

Special Activity C: Driving a Car

Procedure: Notice passing drivers and talk about what they are doing while driving. Also, talk about what passengers can do while riding.

- Discuss Activities of the Day

- Prepare to Leave / Dismissal

DAILY LESSON PLAN 46

Theme: Health—Dentist

- Free Play

Special Activity A: "Numeral Book of Tiny Things"—"Three" [See Table of Contents.]

Lesson Skill 20: Language Development

Objective: To increase vocabulary by naming edible objects

Materials: Paper plates, food and inedible objects

Procedure: Work with the children in small groups. Give each child a plate with both food and inedible items on it. Ask the children to remove all of the items that are not food. Then have each child name the food items that are left on his/her plates. Point out foods which are good for our teeth and bodies.

Lesson Skill 88c: Visual Motor Coordination

Objective: To improve eye-hand coordination by drawing a person

Materials: Chalkboard, chalk, paper, crayons

Procedure: Draw a picture of a person on the chalkboard as the children suggest body parts. Then have each child draw a picture of a person on paper. Write each child's name and the date on his/her paper and file it in the child's individual file folder.

- Handwork: Toothpaste Puzzle

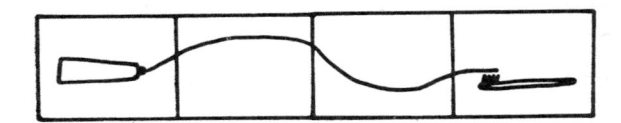

Materials: Four 3" x 5" cards for each child: one with a toothpaste tube drawn on it, another with a toothbrush on it, and two left blank; markers, paper clips

Procedure: Help each child line up his/her cards: toothpaste card first, 2 blank cards next and the toothbrush card last. Show the children how to draw a line from the toothpaste tube across the two blank cards and onto the toothbrush. Explain that the toothpaste line may be a straight line, a wavy line or any way the child chooses to draw it, as long as it ends up on the toothbrush. Then have the children mix up the cards and put them back in the correct order. (Paper clip each child's cards together to take home.)

- Clean Up

- Pre-Story Activities: Weather, Days of Week, Songs, Fingerplays, Sharing Time

Special Activity B: The Tooth Brushing Chart

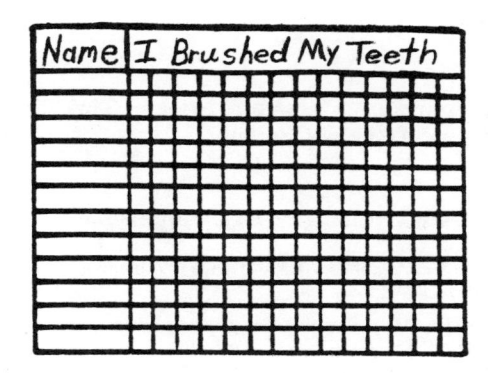

Procedure: Put the "Tooth Brushing Chart" on display. Each child who has brushed his/her teeth that day puts a star by his/her name. (Continue for as many days as desired.)

Special Activity C: Daily Brushing

Procedure: Discuss the importance of brushing every day. Have the children give as many reasons as they can. Unbrushed teeth may develop cavities which could cause toothaches. Clean teeth will be more healthy. People need healthy teeth for chewing food, for speaking clearly and for smiling nicely.

- Story

- Dismiss Group Procedure: Dismiss the children by their shoe classifications: tie, buckle, slip on, velcro closure and others.

- Snack

- Science Experience

- Outside Activities and/or Games

- Discuss Activities of the Day

- Prepare to Leave/Dismissal

DAILY LESSON PLAN 47

Theme: Health—Food

- Free Play

<u>Special Activity A</u>: "Numeral Book of Tiny Things"—"Four" [See Table of Contents.]

Lesson Skill 21: Language Development

Objective: To increase vocabulary by naming foods in the four basic groups

Materials: Magazine pictures of food from each of the four basic food groups, 4 boxes—one with a picture of milk and cheese on it, another with meat and eggs on it, a third with fruit and vegetables on it; and a fourth with bread and cereal on it, 4 sheets of paper showing the same pictures as those on the boxes

Procedure: Sort the pictures of food into the correct boxes. Then working with the children in small groups, have each child pick a picture from each box, say what it is and place it with its corresponding picture on the sheet of paper. Talk about the food group to which it belongs. Continue with all of the children.

Lesson Skill 43c: Memory

Objective: To recall data necessary to name body parts

Materials: Mirror, paper, pencil

Procedure: Work with the children individually. Have each child name as many of his/her body parts as possible. For clarity and reinforcement, try using a mirror in which both teacher and child can point out and see the various parts. Record the date and the body parts that each child names. File the list in the child's individual file folder.

- Handwork: A Balanced Meal

Materials: Paper plates, magazine pictures of food from the four basic food groups, glue

Procedure: Give each child a paper plate. Place the pictures from one food group on the table. Each child chooses one and glues it onto a portion of his plate. Remove the unused pictures. Continue in the same way with the remaining 3 food groups. Discuss each group.

- Clean Up

- Pre-Story Activities: Weather, Days of Week, Songs, Fingerplays, Sharing Time

<u>Special Activity B</u>: Good Food

Procedure: Lead a discussion about foods with high nutritional value, such as nuts, seeds, fruits, vegetables, milk products, and meat. Have the children suggest other good foods. Explain that good food helps them to be healthy and grow bigger and stronger.

- Story

- Dismiss Group Procedure: Give each child a food picture. Name the food group to which the food belongs. Have the children leave when they recognize the name of the food group to which their food belongs. Help the children to determine their food groups by naming the food groups and other similar foods in them.

- Snack

- Science Experience

- Outside Activities and/or Games

- Discuss Activities of the Day

- Prepare to Leave / Dismissal

Daily Lesson Plans 61

DAILY LESSON PLAN 48

Theme: Special Holidays

- Free Play

Special Activity A: "Numeral Book of Tiny Things" — "Five" [See Table of Contents.]

Lesson Skill 45: Memory

Objective: To recall data necessary to retell events

Materials: A doll or puppet and appropriate props (example: for St. Patrick's Day — a leprechaun doll and a pot of gold)

Procedure: Working with each child individually, tell a story with three action parts, such as: "I was chasing a leprechaun. I caught him. He showed me where his pot of gold was hidden." Then have the child tell the story. Record the number of action parts recalled and the order in which they were said. (If the story is mixed up or incomplete, do not correct the child verbally. Have him/her act out the story while the teacher repeats it (and animates the doll). Then have the child repeat the story.

Lesson Skill 78c: Gross Motor Coordination

Objective: To improve large muscle abilities by throwing and catching a ball

Materials: A ball, 8" or larger

Procedure: At a distance of from 4 to 8 feet, have each child throw the ball to the Teacher and then catch it. Repeat the exchange several times to determine the child's level of skill and to have fun. Record the level for the child's individual file. Compare with earlier performance. (May be done during "Outside" time.)

- **Handwork: Cup and Ball Catcher**

Materials: Styrofoam cups and 1 1/2" styrofoam balls, 24" pieces of yarn, a long needle, special holiday decorations cut from paper (sized to fit on the cups), glue

Procedure: Thread a length of yarn through the needle. Then knot an end and pull the needle and yarn through the bottom of the cup, from inside to outside. Next, pull the needle and yarn through the styrofoam ball, remove the needle, and tie a large knot in the other end of the yarn (to link the cup and the ball). Have the children glue the holiday decorations onto their cups. Finally, have the children practice using their "cup-and-ball catchers".

- Clean Up

- Pre-Story Activities: Weather, Days of Week, Songs, Fingerplays, Sharing Time

Special Activity B: Featured Holiday

Procedure: Discuss the history of the featured holiday. Explain why people remember to celebrate the holiday. Discuss any customs associated with the holiday. Tell about their origins.

- Story

- Dismiss Group Procedure: Scatter two similar, yet slightly different, sets of holiday symbols on the floor. (Example: three leaf and four leaf green paper clovers for St. Patrick's Day.) Dismiss each child as he/she finds an example of the symbol, designated by the Teacher. (Be sure to have more than enough of the designated symbols for all the children in the group.)

- Snack

- Science Experience

- Outside Activities and/or Games

- Discuss Activities of the Day

- Prepare to Leave / Dismissal

DAILY LESSON PLAN 49

Theme: Spring

- Free Play

Special Activity A: "Numeral Book of Tiny Things"— "Six" [See Table of Contents.]

Lesson Skill 18: Language Development

Objective: To increase vocabulary by naming spring items

Materials: Buds from trees, a kite, pussy willows, crocuses or other early spring flowers, a rain coat, a soccer ball, a baseball and a bat

Procedure: Have the children meet as a group. Explain that all the objects on the table are associated with spring. Have each child pick up an object from the table and say, "This is a _____."

Lesson Skill 42c: Memory

Objective: To recall data necessary to name colors

Materials: Color Wheel

Procedure: Working with each child individually, point to the colors on the color wheel. Ask the child to identify the colors. Record any unfamiliar colors. Help the child to learn the names and recognize the unfamiliar colors by pointing out objects in the room that are those colors. Emphasize one or two new colors.

- **Handwork: Pussy Willow Pictures**

Materials: Light to medium colored green construction paper (8 1/2" x 11"), brown felt markers, white paint, paint shirts

Procedure: Have the children draw branches on their papers. Then have each child dip a finger in the white paint and dab it onto the branches to make pussy willows.

- Clean Up

- Pre-Story Activities: Weather, Days of Week, Songs, Fingerplays, Sharing Time

Special Activity B: Season Dial

Procedure: Show the Season Dial. Talk about each picture and have the children find the current season. (Activity works best on a spring-like day.) Talk about spring weather, spring clothing, plants, trees in the spring, spring sports and baby animals. Ask the children what they like to do in the spring.

- Story

- Dismiss Group Procedure: Write the initials of the children's first names on individual construction paper kites. Then dismiss the children as they recognize their initials.

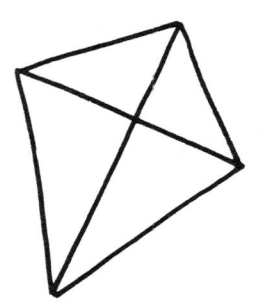

- Snack

- Science Experience

- Outside Activities and/or Games

Special Activity C: Buds

Procedure: Have the children look for buds on trees.

- Discuss Activities of the Day

- Prepare to Leave / Dismissal

DAILY LESSON PLAN 50

Theme: Spring

- Free Play

<u>Special Activity A</u>: "Numeral Book of Tiny Things" — "Seven" [See Table of Contents.]

Lesson Skill 61: Visual Discrimination

Objective: To perceive and express relationships of various states of matter

Materials: 3 equal-sized pans containing equal amounts of water (one frozen solid and two liquid), a burner, a freezer

Procedure:

Step #1: As the children watch, mark the level of the frozen water on the pan. Then remove the ice for the children to hold in their hands and feel its solidity. Next, have them discuss solid, liquid and gas as separate states of matter. Ask if ice is liquid or solid or gas. Next, melt the ice in the pan. Then compare the solid ice level mark to the liquid water level.

Step #2: Have the children pour the liquid water into containers of various shapes. Have them note that water is a liquid. Talk about other things that are liquids. Ask if water is solid or liquid or gas. Discuss the fact that the shape of a liquid depends on the shape of its container.

Step #3: Mark the level of the water in the third pan. Change the liquid water into steam, a gas, by putting it on a burner. Show the children the steam (be cautious that no one gets close enough to the pan or steam to get burned). Explain that the water has turned into steam, a gas (actually little bits of water hanging in the air). Ask them if the steam is solid or liquid or gas. Let the water boil a few minutes, then carefully measure the water level in the pan. Let the children observe that there is less water now because some of it turned into steam and is now in the air.

Lesson Skill 41c: Memory

Objective: To recall data necessary to answer story questions

Materials: Storybook

Procedure: Read a story aloud and ask each child to answer questions about it. Start with questions about characters, and then go on to sequence and plot. Record the response level. (May be done during "Story".)

- Handwork: Weather Dial
  [See Table of Contents]

Materials: Weather pictures, heavy construction paper or cardboard (11" x 11"), a pointer (1" x 5") cut from heavy construction paper or cardboard, scissors, glue, crayons, brads

Procedure: Have each child cut out and glue weather pictures onto the heavy paper. Help him/her to attach a pointer with a brad. Have the children color the weather pictures.

- Clean Up

- Pre-Story Activities: Weather, Days of Week, Songs, Fingerplays, Sharing Time

<u>Special Activity B</u>: Weather Dials

Procedure: Have the children hold their weather dials and move the pointer to the same pictures. Talk about the kind of weather depicted. Continue with the remaining weather picture. Have the children decide where to point their pointers to indicate today's weather. Suggest that they point out the weather each day at home.

<u>Special Activity C</u>: Fall and Spring

Procedure: Present a pile of fall and spring pictures and tell the children that some are fall pictures and others are spring pictures. Have each child pick out a picture, tell which season it shows and tell why he/she thinks it is that season.

- Story

- Dismiss Group Procedure: Dismiss the children as they recognize their names on flowers. Read names aloud for children who do not recognize them.

- Snack

- Science Experience

- Outside Activities and/or Games

- Discuss Activities of the Day

- Prepare to Leave / Dismissal

DAILY LESSON PLAN 51

Theme: Spring — April Fool's Day

- Free Play

Special Activity A: "Numeral Book of Tiny Things" — "Eight" [See Table of Contents.]

Lesson Skill 68: Visual Discrimination

Objective: To increase visual perception by identifying what does not belong in a picture

Materials: Lesson Sheet, crayons

Procedure: The children circle the part of the picture that is wrong.

Lesson Skill 87c: Visual-Motor Coordination

Objective: To develop eye-hand coordination by writing name

Materials: Paper, pencil

Procedure: Have each child write as much of his/her name as possible. Date and place these papers in the individual file folders. (Encourage the children to write their names on their daily projects.)

- Handwork: April Fool

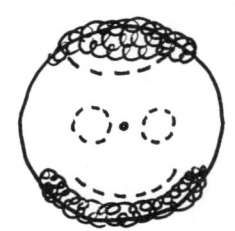

Materials: Pre-drawn April Fool face, crayons

Procedure: Have the children connect the dots to draw the April Fool's face. Then have them add hair and a beard. Show that the face is happy when held one way and sad when it is turned upside down.

- Clean Up

- Pre-Story Activities: Weather, Days of Week, Songs, Fingerplays, Sharing Time

Special Activity B: April Fool Jokes

Procedure: Discuss April Fool's jokes. Tell the children that this is one day of the year when they can fool people by saying things that are not true. But right afterwards they must say, "April Fool!", so people will know that they were just joking, and not lying.

- Story

- Dismiss Group Procedure: Dismiss the children as they recognize the initials of their first names on butterflies.

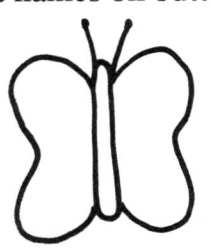

- Snack

- Science Experience

- Outside Activities and/or Games

- Discuss Activities of the Day

Special Activity C: Parents' April Fool

Procedure: Have the children get ready to go home a few minutes early. Then have them hide in the room. When the parents come, tell each one, "I am sorry but child's name is not here. He/she went to California" (or some other far away place). At this moment, have the child come out of hiding and say "April Fool!". (Secretly let the parents in on the joke beforehand. Don't worry them, even momentarily.)

- Prepare to Leave / Dismissal

Daily Lesson Plans

DAILY LESSON PLAN 52

Theme: Spring

- Free Play

Special Activity A: "Numeral Book of Tiny Things" — "Nine" [See Table of Contents.]

Lesson Skill 24: Language Development

Objective: To learn directional terms such as on, off, in and out

Materials: A spring flower basket with a cover, a plastic flower

Procedure: Working with each child individually, tell him/her to 1) put the flower on the cover of the basket, 2) take the flower off the cover, 3) put the flower in the basket, and 4) take the flower out of the basket. Then repeat all of the above movement activities, and have the child tell where the flower is in relation to the basket.

Lesson Skill 34c: Language Development

Objective: To enhance correct word pronunciation by saying initial sounds clearly

Materials: Initial Sound Cards, Pocket Chart [See Table of Contents]

Procedure: Working with each child individually, have him/her pick up the cards one at a time from the pile, say what the pictures show, and then place the cards on the pocket chart. The child might not say the desired response. If so, agree with any correct word and say, "It is also _____. Say that for me." Note and record any mispronounced sounds.

- Handwork: Bunny Puppet

Materials: Paper plates, blue or brown eyes, pink noses, and white ears cut from construction paper, pipe cleaners, craft sticks, glue and pink crayons

Procedure: Have the children color the insides of the ears pink. Then have each child glue a set of ears, eyes and a nose along with pipe cleaner whiskers onto a paper plate. Next, have the child draw a pink crayon mouth on the bunny's face. Finally, have him/her glue a craft stick onto the back of the plate for use as a holder for the puppet.

- Clean Up

- Pre-Story Activities: Weather, Days of Week, Songs, Fingerplays, Sharing Time

Special Activity B: Empty/Full

Procedure: Place a crayon in one plastic egg and leave another egg empty. (Tape both eggs shut.) Then have each child shake the eggs to determine which is empty and which is not.

- Story

- Dismiss Group Procedure: Show pre-cut paper flowers in various solid colors and identify each color. Then dismiss the children as they recognize flowers in the same color as their clothing.

- Snack

- Science Experience

- Outside Activities and/or Games

Special Activity C: Cloud Forms

Procedure: Have the children look at the clouds. Discuss the cloud shapes and what they resemble. (Any flowers, bunnies, eggs, baskets?) Encourage a variety of ideas.

- Discuss Activities of the Day

- Prepare to Leave / Dismissal

DAILY LESSON PLAN 53

Theme: Spring

- Free Play

Special Activity A: "Numeral Book of Tiny Things" — "Ten" [See Table of Contents.]

Lesson Skill 75: Visual Discrimination

Objective: To increase visual perception by matching: 1) object to object, 2) object to picture, 3) picture to picture

Materials: 1) groups of 3 or 4 related toys, (plus one which is of a different classification), 2) photographs of actual objects in the classroom, 3) Lesson Sheet, crayon

Procedure: Work with each child individually. 1) Place 3 or 4 identical toys on a table (plus one that is different) and have the child group the toys which are the same. Repeat with other sets of toys. 2) Give the child 3 pictures of objects found in the classroom. Have him/her find the actual objects. 3) On the lesson sheet, have the child circle the pictures that are the same as the one shown in the box.

Lesson Skill 85c: Visual-Motor Coordination

Objective: To develop eye-hand coordination by connecting dots on angular and curved lines

Materials: Lesson Sheet, pencils

Procedure: Have the children connect the dots to complete the chick picture. They may then color their pictures.

- **Handwork: Flowers in Pots**

  Materials: Styrofoam cups, crayons, flower cutouts, straws, glue, scrap paper

  Procedure: Have the children draw designs and/or pictures on the cups with crayons. Have them glue flowers to the ends of straws. Have them crumple the scrap paper and put it into the cups. Then have them stick the straw ends (stems of their flowers) into the crumpled paper (dirt) in the pots.

- Clean Up

- Pre-Story Activities: Weather, Days of Week, Songs, Fingerplays, Sharing Time

Special Activity B: Bunny Tail Game

Procedure: Place a large picture of a bunny (rear or side view) on a wall. Have the children who wish to play take turns wearing a blindfold, walking the few steps to the bunny and trying to stick a cotton ball (with rolled tape on it) onto the bunny. See who puts the cotton ball closest to the tail spot.

- Story

- Dismiss Group Procedure: Show pre-cut paper flowers in various solid colors and identify each color. Then dismiss the children as they recognize flowers in the same color as their clothing.

- Snack

- Science Experience

- Outside Activities and/or Games

- Discuss Activities of the Day

- Prepare to Leave / Dismissal

Daily Lesson Plans

DAILY LESSON PLAN 54

Theme: Spring

- **Free Play**

Special Activity A: "Numeral Book of Tiny Things"— Compilation [See Table of Contents.]

Lesson Skill 70: Visual Discrimination

Objective: To increase visual perception by finding hidden pictures

Materials: Lesson sheet, crayons

Procedure: Point out the picture in the box. Have the children find and mark the hidden pictures like the one in the box.

Lesson Skill 39c: Memory

Objective: To recall data necessary to follow directions

Procedure: Give three activity directions to each child.

Examples:

1) Put eggs in a basket.
2) Hop like a bunny.
3) Wiggle your nose like a bunny.

1) Pick some spring flowers.
2) Put on a bonnet.
3) Pretend you are a chick coming out of a shell.

1) Carry an egg basket to the table.
2) Give an egg to me.
3) Draw an egg on the chalkboard.

1) Frost spring cookies.
2) Hide eggs in the room.
3) Hug a stuffed bunny.

Reorder directions each time so that the children cannot imitate what someone else has done. Note and record the number of directions each child follows.

- **Handwork: Twin Chicks**

  Materials: Egg shell halves (washed), cotton balls, glue, yellow paint powder, felt markers

  Procedure: Have the children glue two cotton balls together and roll them around in the yellow paint powder. Then have them use felt markers to draw eyes, nose and mouth on one ball, and then glue it on top of the other ball. Finally, have the children glue the balls into an egg shell half.

- **Clean Up**

- **Pre-Story Activities:** Weather, Days of Week, Songs, Fingerplays, Sharing Time

  Special Activity B: Pretend Bunnies

  Procedure: Have the children pretend that they are bunnies. Have them put on their imaginary bunny suits and zip them up. Then have them "feel" their soft fur and long ears. Also, have them stroke their whiskers and wiggle their noses. Then have them hop around and pretend to look for carrots. Finally, have them "change" themselves back into children again.

- **Story**

- **Dismiss Group Procedure:** Show pre-cut paper eggs in various solid colors and identify each color. Then dismiss the children as they recognize eggs in the same color as their clothing.

- **Snack**

- **Science Experience**

- **Outside Activities and/or Games**

- **Discuss Activities of the Day**

- **Prepare to Leave / Dismissal**

DAILY LESSON PLAN 55

Theme: Day And Night

- Free Play

Special Activity A: "Book of Feelings" — "Happy" [See Table of Contents.]

Lesson Skill 33: Language Development

Objective: To increase listening comprehension through recognizing opposites

Procedure: Have each child complete the following sentences:

It is dark at night and light during the _____. (day)

We are awake during the day and at night we _____. (sleep)

We see the sun during the day and at night we see the _____. (moon or stars) It is cold in the winter and in the summer it is _____. (hot)

When we laugh we are happy and when we cry we are _____. (sad)

(Accept any reasonable answer. Supply answers if he/she does not know them. Also, state the sentences again, reversing their order and omitting another part of each, so the child will have more practice recognizing opposites. For your records, count only the answers that the child comes up with on his/her own).

Lesson Skill 55c: Math Readiness

Objective: To establish a basis for understanding math by naming numbers

Procedure: Ask each child, individually, to count as high as possible.

- Handwork: Awake/Asleep Necklace

Materials: Construction paper circles 4" in diameter, paper punch, yarn, felt markers

Procedure: Have each child draw the face of an awake person on one side of his/her circle and of an asleep person on the other side. Label the faces "Awake" and "Asleep." Have the child punch a hole in the top of the circle and tie yarn through it to make a necklace.

- Clean Up

- Pre-Story Activities: Weather, Days of Week, Songs, Fingerplays, Sharing Time

Special Activity B: Day and Night

Procedure: Show day and night pictures to the class and talk about the differences between the two. Have the children discuss daytime things and nighttime things that they like to do. Also, make lists of the opposite qualities of day and night.

- Story

- Dismiss Group Procedure: Dismiss the children as they recognize the initials of their first names written on paper moons.

- Snack

- Science Experience

- Outside Activities and/or Games

Special Activity C: Sunlight

Procedure: Talk about the sun's daytime light and warmth.

- Discuss Activities of the Day

- Prepare to Leave / Dismissal

Daily Lesson Plans

DAILY LESSON PLAN 56

Theme: Farm

- Free Play

Special Activity A: "Book of Feelings" — "Sad"
[See Table of Contents.]

Lesson Skill 9: Language Development

Objective: To construct sentences using negatives in the middle

Materials: Working with each child individually, say positive sentences that are not true. Then have the children repeat the sentences making them into negative sentences

Positive Examples:

Turkeys have four feet.
Eggs come from donkeys.
Baby chicks come from pigs.
Pigs are skinny.
Pigs say "Peep! Peep!"
Ducks are red.
Ham comes from turkeys.
Horses fly.
Roosters like to swim.
Goats live in houses.

Lesson Skill 56c: Math Readiness

Objective: To establish a basis for understanding math by counting objects

Materials: Plastic farm animals

Procedure: Work with the children individually. Instruct each child to count as many of the animals as he or she can. Have the child touch the animals as he or she says each number. (Be sure the child works from left to right to aid correct eye-hand coordination.)

- Handwork: Farm Animals

Materials: Construction paper and the pre-cut heads and tails of several different animals made from construction paper

Procedure: Have the children choose a head and tail set and draw bodies and legs to complete them. Then have them glue the heads and tails to their drawings.

- Clean Up

- Pre-Story Activities: Weather, Days of Week, Songs, Fingerplays, Sharing Time

Special Activity B: Animal Tales

Procedure: Display plastic animals in a box or barn. Have the children, one at a time, select an animal, identify it and tell what sound it makes.

- Story

- Dismiss Group Procedure: Dismiss the children as they recognize a word or sound that rhymes with their names. (If available, use a farm animal puppet to say rhyming words or sounds.)

- Snack

- Science Experience

- Outside Activities and/or Games

Special Activity C: Animals Outside

Procedure: Notice animals when outside. Listen for their sounds.

- Discuss Activities of the Day

- Prepare to Leave / Dismissal

DAILY LESSON PLAN 57

Theme: Farm

- Free Play

Special Activity A: "Book of Feelings" — "Proud" [See Table of Contents.]

Lesson Skill 11: Language Development

Objective: To construct sentences using adverbs

Procedure: Working with each child individually, say a sentence and ask the child a question to help him/her pick out the adverbs. Then have the child repeat the sentence using the adverb.

Sample sentences and questions:

1) The piglets were born yesterday.
   When were the piglets born?
2) The dog barked loudly.
   How did the dog bark?
3) The farmer's family happily ate their dinner.
   How did the farmer's family eat their dinner?
4) The rooster quickly chased the mouse.
   How did the rooster chase the mouse?
5) The donkey would not move today.
   When would the donkey not move?
6) The farmer's wife was very angry when the goat chewed up part of the laundry.
   How angry was the farmer's wife?

Lesson Skill 83c: Fine Motor Coordination

Objective: To improve small muscle abilities by cutting on straight and curved lines.

Materials: Stand-up pig, crayons, scissors

Procedure: Have the children cut on the heavy lines and fold on the dotted lines to make stand-up pigs. Note their cutting ability on both straight and curved lines. (Be sure to give left-handed scissors to children who are left-handed.)

- Handwork: Hen

Materials: Cellophane grass, corn kernels, paper, a hen and 3 eggs drawn on paper, scissors, crayons, glue, 8 1/2" x 11" paper.

Procedure: Have each child color and cut out the hen and the eggs. Then have him/her glue the grass onto the paper (to make a nest) and glue the corn kernels outside the grass nest. Next, have him/her glue the hen next to the nest (eating corn) and glue the eggs inside the nest.

- Clean Up

- Pre-Story Activities: Weather, Days of Week, Sharing Time

Special Activity B: Hens and Eggs

Procedure: Have the children discuss hens' liking for corn, the laying and hatching of eggs and the various colors of hens — brown, white, black, gray. (Point out the uses of eggs and chickens for food.)

Special Activity C: Pigs

Procedure: Using the stand-up pig (from Lesson Skill 83c), lead into a discussion of pigs, their color variations — white, pink, black and gray, their liking for corn and vegetables and especially their need for mud wallowing (body heat regulation).

(Point out the uses of pork for food.)

- Story

- Dismiss Group Procedure: Dismiss the children as they recognize the initial of their first name written on an animal footprint.

Daily Lesson Plans

- Snack

- Science Experience

- Outside Activities and/or Games

<u>Special Activity D</u>: Pig Trail

>Procedure: Have the children follow the pig footprints until they come to the picture of a pig.

- Discuss Activities of the Day

- Prepare to Leave / Dismissal

DAILY LESSON PLAN 58

Theme: Farm

- Free Play

Special Activity A: "Book of Feelings" — "Sorry" [See Table of Contents.]

Lesson Skill 69: Visual Discrimination

Objective: To increase visual perception by continuing dot patterns

Materials: Lesson sheets, pictures of animals, tape, crayons

Procedure: Have the children choose animal pictures, one each, and tape them onto their lesson sheets. Then have the children connect the dots on the sheets to make fences for their animal.

Lesson Skill 86c: Visual-Motor Coordination

Objective: To develop eye-hand coordination by copying a square, a circle, and a triangle

Materials: Paper, pencil

Procedure: Working with each child individually, draw a square on the paper. Ask him/her to draw a second square on this paper. Continue in the same manner with circles and triangles. Date these papers and place them in the children's individual file folders.

- Handwork: Animal Puzzles

Materials: Magazine pictures of farm animals, rubber cement, construction paper on which lines are drawn for puzzle parts, scissors, paper clips

Procedure: Have the children glue the backs of the animal pictures to the blank side of the construction paper. Then have them cut along the lines drawn on the back of the construction paper, thereby making puzzle pieces. Give the children time to put their puzzles together, then save the pieces in individual envelopes.

- Clean Up

- Pre-Story Activities: Weather, Days of Week, Songs, Fingerplays, Sharing Time

Special Activity B: Farm Animals

Procedure: Have each child choose a picture of a farm animal. One at a time, have him/her imitate the animal's behavior and its sounds. Have the other children try to guess the animal's identity.

- Story

- Dismiss Group Procedure: Have each child choose an animal footprint. Dismiss each child as he/she recognizes matching footprints.

- Snack

- Science Experience

- Outside Activities and/or Games

- Discuss Activities of the Day

- Prepare to Leave / Dismissal

DAILY LESSON PLAN 59

Theme: Zoo Animals

- Free Play

Special Activity A: "Book of Feelings" — "Brave" [See Table of Contents.]

Lesson Skill 27: Language Development

Objective: To increase listening comprehension through yes/no nonsense questions

Materials: Magazine pictures of zoo animals (kangaroo, leopard, lion, tiger, monkey, bear, elephant, camel, zebra, giraffe, lama, and others), a list of questions about the animals

Procedure: Work with each child individually. Show him/her one animal picture at a time and ask nonsense questions about the animals. (Note: The child's responses will show whether or not he/she understands the questions.

Examples of nonsense questions:

Do kangaroos live in trees?
Are tigers pink?
Are elephants smaller than mice?
Do lions wear sweaters?
Is a zebra shaped like a pig?
Do camels fly?
Does a giraffe have a neck?
Do monkeys live underground?
Does a llama have two tails?
Can bears talk like people?
Do leopards have black and white stripes?

Lesson Skill 40c: Memory

Objective: To recall the data necessary to repeat a series of numbers and a series of words

Procedure: Working with each child individually, have him/her listen to and repeat numbers. Start with 1/2 second intervals, building to 2 seconds between numbers. Start with a sequence of 2 numbers. When this is mastered, go on to a sequence of 3. Keep adding one more number to find out how many they are able to recall. Give at least three examples for each sequence. Do the same with words. Include zoo words: zoo, caretaker, kangaroo, leopard, tiger, lion, monkey, bear, elephant, camel, zebra, giraffe.

- Handwork: Bears

Materials: A drawing of a bear on 8 1/2" x 11" paper, glue, ground coffee, pre-cut construction paper eyes, nose and mouth, scissors

Procedure: Have the children cover the bears with glue, then sprinkle on some coffee and shake off the excess. Next, glue on the bear's eyes, nose and mouth. Finally, after it is completely dry, cut out the bear.

- Clean Up

- Pre-Story Activities: Weather, Days of Week, Songs, Fingerplays, Sharing Time

Special Activity B: Zoo Animals

Procedure: (Cut pictures of zoo animals in half.) Give a half of a picture to each child and display the pictures' other halves on a tabletop. Have the children locate the matching halves for their pictures. Next, have them sit down and tell about the animals in their pictures. Also, have them point out and name a special feature of each of their animals.

- Story

- Dismiss Group Procedure: Dismiss the children as they recognize their names written on paper bears. Read names aloud for those who do not recognize them.

- Snack

- Science Experience

- Outside Activities and/or Games

- Discuss Activities of the Day

- Prepare to Leave / Dismissal

DAILY LESSON PLAN 60

Theme: May Day

- Free Play

<u>Special Activity A</u>: "Book of Feelings" — "Hurt" [See Table of Contents.]

Lesson Skill 14: Language Development

Objective: To construct sentences using relative clauses

Materials: Magazine pictures of forest animal mothers (deer, fox, squirrel, raccoon rabbit, porcupine, chipmunk, skunk), pictures of their babies, pictures of flowers, pocket chart

Procedure: Working with each child individually, have him/her choose three pictures (one showing flowers, one showing an animal mother, and one showing an animal baby). Have him/her place the pictures on the pocket chart. Then say, for example, "The bunny brought flowers to his mother, who ____." Have the child finish the sentence by saying something that the mother animal might do because she received flowers from her baby. Repeat the completed sentence and then have the child say it again.

Lesson Skill 79c: Gross Motor Coordination

Objective: To improve large muscle abilities by using alternate feet to walk down steps

Materials: Steps

Procedure: Work with the children in small groups. Show them how to alternate their feet while walking down steps. Encourage each child to do this. Note and record their coordination levels.

- Handwork: May Baskets

Materials: Small (3 1/2" x 6 1/2") envelopes (with cutout area marked), flowers drawn on various colors of construction paper, 6" green pipe cleaners, scissors, tape, crayons

Procedure: Have the children seal their envelopes and then cut out the marked areas. (They may need help.) Then have them decorate the envelopes by coloring pictures or designs. Next, have them cut out the flower outlines and tape them to the ends of pipe cleaner stems. Finally, insert the pipe cleaner stems into the baskets.

- Clean Up

- Pre-Story Activities: Weather, Days of Week, Songs, Fingerplays, Sharing Time

<u>Special Activity B</u>: May Basket Delivery

Procedure: Discuss clever ways for the children to deliver May baskets to their recipients. For example, the giver could hang the basket of flowers on a doorknob or place it on the steps by the door, then ring the doorbell and hide. When the recipient discovers the basket, the giver would jump out from hiding and say, "Happy May Day" to the recipient.

- Story

- Dismiss Group Procedure: Draw 2 flowers on one 4" x 5" index card, 3 flowers on another, 4 on another, 5 on another, and write the number of flowers on each card. Dismiss the children as they see and identify the card with the number of flowers which is the same as their individual ages.

- Snack

- Science Experience

- Outside Activities and/or Games

- Discuss Activities of the Day

- Prepare to Leave / Dismissal

Daily Lesson Plans

DAILY LESSON PLAN 61

Theme: Special Family Days

- Free Play

Special Activity A: "Book of Feelings" — "Excited" [See Table of Contents.]

Lesson Skill 50: Math Readiness

Objective: To establish a basis for understanding math by matching corresponding objects

Materials: Pictures of 4 mother frogs, 4 baby tadpoles and 4 lily pads, cut from construction paper

Procedure: Work with each child individually. On a tabletop, place a mother frog on each lily pad. Also, place the tadpoles nearby. Ask the child to help each tadpole to go to its mother.

Lesson Skill 80c: Gross Motor Coordination

Objective: To improve large muscle abilities by walking backwards, walking on a balance board and standing on each foot

Materials: Balance board

Procedure: Working with each child individually, show him/her how to walk backwards for six steps, to walk forward on a balance board and to stand on each foot for five seconds. Note and record the coordination level of each child.

- Handwork: Napkin Holders (for Mother's Day presents)

Materials: Liquid laundry detergent bottles (32 oz. size), dish pan of water, towels, felt markers, scissors

Procedure: (Several hours earlier) have each child place a bottle in the dish pan of water (to soak off the labels). After the bottle is peeled and dried, outline the child's hand print on both sides of the bottle. Next, cut out the hand prints, leaving the bottom of the bottle still attached (to form a base and to join the hand prints together). Have the children use the felt markers to draw designs or pictures on the hands.

Special Activity B: Mother's Day Card

Materials: Cupcake papers, crayons, 8 1/2" x 11" paper folded in half

Procedure: (Write "Happy Mother's Day" on the fronts of all the cards; also, on the inside of the cards, write dot-to-dot letters to spell "I love you.") Have the children glue the cupcake paper "flowers" onto the fronts of their cards. Then have them use crayons to draw stems and leaves for their flowers. Next, have them connect the dots (inside the cards) to spell "I love you" and draw pictures or other decorations. Finally, have them sign their names (give help if necessary). (Be sensitive to children who do not have mothers. They can make cards for some other special person in their lives.)

- Clean Up

- Pre-Story Activities: Weather, Days of Week, Songs, Fingerplays, Sharing Time

Special Activity C: Mothers Are Special

Procedure: Have the children think of ways in which their mothers (or other people) are special, some things their mothers do that they really like. Write each child's ideas inside his/her Mother's Day card.

- Story

- Dismiss Group Procedure: Dismiss the children as they recognize their initials on frogs.

- Snack

- Science Experience

- Outside Activities and/or Games

- Discuss Activities of the Day

- Prepare to Leave / Dismissal

DAILY LESSON PLAN 62

Theme: Natural Environment

- Free Play

Special Activity A: "Book of Feelings" — "Bored" [See Table of Contents.]

Lesson Skill 58: Math Readiness

Objective: To establish a basis for understanding math by thinking back to earlier states

Materials: Pictures of flowers, plants, trees, prepared foods (mashed potatoes, sliced carrots, diced beets, fried egg), objects made from wood, woven baskets

Procedure: Working with each child individually, show him/her one picture at a time and ask how the subject of the picture looked before it was, for example, a flower. Try questions such as, "From where did it come?", "What are its parts?" and "What was it before?" Record the children's answers.

Lesson Skill 89c: Visual-Motor Coordination

Objective: To develop eye-hand coordination by using left-to-right progression and top-to-bottom progression

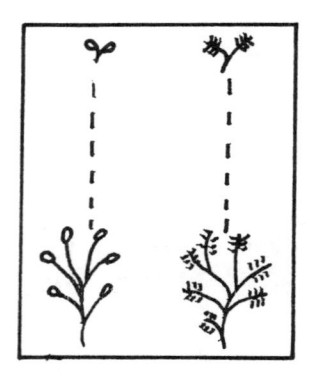

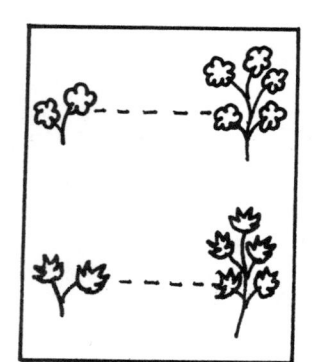

Materials: Two lesson sheets for each child, one for left-to-right progression and one for top-to-bottom progression, pencils

Procedure: One lesson sheet at a time, instruct the children to draw lines from the smaller plants to the larger ones.

- **Handwork: Leaf Collage**

Materials: Real leaves, large sheets of paper, glue

Procedure: Have the children glue the leaves onto the paper to make a picture or design.

- Clean Up

- Pre-Story Activities: Weather, Days of Week, Songs, Fingerplays, Sharing Time

Special Activity B: Planting

Procedure: Have the children pantomime the planting process. (Dig a hole, put the seed in, cover it, and water it.) Also, discuss the natural environment; explain how trees grow from seeds, too. If possible, plant a tree at school and/or send seedlings home with the children for planting.

- Story

- Dismiss Group Procedure: (Cut out paper flowers of all colors.) Dismiss the children as they recognize the colors of their clothing as being the same as the colors of the flowers.

- Snack

- Science Experience

- Outside Activities and/or Games

Procedure: Before the children go outside, make a trail of real or paper leaves leading to a tree with the same kind of leaves. Once outside, have the children follow the trail.

- Discuss Activities of the Day

- Prepare to Leave / Dismissal

DAILY LESSON PLAN 63

Theme: Plants

- Free Play

Special Activity A: "Book of Feelings" – "Safe" [See Table of Contents.]

Lesson Skill 71: Visual Discrimination

Objective: To increase visual perception by finding hidden shapes

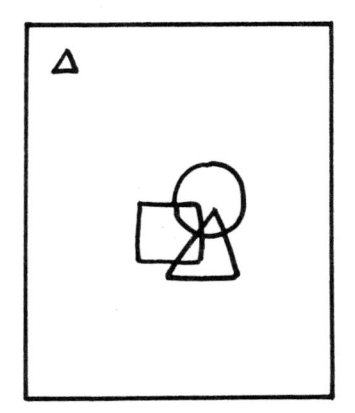

Materials: Lesson sheet, crayons

Procedure: Point to the triangle at the top of the page and ask the children to find one in the picture and outline it with their crayons.

Lesson Skill 81c: Fine Motor Coordination

Objective: To improve small muscle abilities by buttoning and tying

Materials: Shirts with buttons (larger buttons for younger children), shoes with laces

Procedure: Work with the children in small groups. Show them how to put a button through a button hole. Then have each child try it. Continue with tying knots and tying bows. Encourage the children to try these skills. However, do not push if the children are not ready.

- Handwork: Plant Screen Painting

Materials: Flowers, leaves, stems, small window screens with masking tape around the edges, paint, paint brushes, paint shirts, paper (8 1/2" x 11")

Procedure: Have the children choose flowers and leaves and arrange them in designs on their papers. Then have them place the screens over their designs and apply paint over everything. Remove the screen and the plant parts and allow the paint to dry. Finally, have the children observe the variety of designs.

- Clean Up

- Pre-Story Activities: Weather, Days of Week, Songs, Fingerplays, Sharing Time

Special Activity B: Lead the class in imitating the growth stages of a plant.

- Story

- Dismiss Group Procedure: Draw a large leaf on the chalkboard. Write various ages on the leaf. Dismiss the children as they recognize their own ages.

- Snack

- Science Experience

- Outside Activities and/or Games

Special Activity C: Gardening

Procedure: Have garden tools outside for the children to use in the sandbox. (Include hoes, spades, rakes, shovels.)

- Discuss Activities of the Day

- Prepare to Leave / Dismissal

DAILY LESSON PLAN 64

Theme: Plants

- Free Play

Special Activity A: "Book of Feelings" — "Afraid" [See Table of Contents.]

Lesson Skill 57: Math Readiness

Objective: To establish a basis for understanding math by comprehending the permanence of numbers

Materials: Felt board, felt bush, 10 felt flowers cover sheet

Procedure: Work with each child individually. Place 2 flowers on the bush. Have the children count the flowers. Then cover the flowers and have the children tell how many flowers are on the bush. Remove the sheet and count the flowers with them to help them check their responses. Continue in this manner, increasing the number of flowers each time as far as the number 10 to help them advance in this skill. Stop where they seem to lack confidence and work with them at this level.

Lesson Skill 82c: Fine Motor Coordination

Objective: To improve small muscle abilities by zipping and snapping clothing

Materials: Jacket with a good working zipper, jacket with snaps (jackets in adult and child sizes)

Procedure: Work with the children in small groups. Show them how to zip and unzip the jacket while wearing it. Then have them try. Continue with snapping. Encourage them to master these skills, but do not push if they are not ready.

- Handwork: Terrariums

Materials: Baby food jars with covers, potting soil, small plants, paper circles the size of the jar covers, felt markers, glue, water

Procedure: Have the children fill the jars about 1/3 full with potting soil. Then have them put their plants in the jars and sprinkle them with water. (An eye-dropper works well.) Next, have them draw pictures or designs on the paper circles and glue them onto the jar covers. Finally, have them put the covers on the jars. (The plants should grow without adding more water.)

- Clean Up

- Pre-Story Activities: Weather, Days of Week, Songs, Fingerplays, Sharing Time

Special Activity B: Flowers Same/Different

Procedure: Have as many different kinds of flowers or pictures of flowers as possible. Show two at a time and talk about how they are the same and how they are different.

- Story

- Dismiss Group Procedure: Display a large picture of a tree on a bulletin board. Show the children cut-out tree leaves on which their names are written. Dismiss each child individually as he/she recognizes his/her name on a leaf and then tacks it onto the tree. Read the names aloud for those children who do not recognize them.

- Snack

- Science Experience

- Outside Activities and/or Games

Special Activity C: Seeds

Procedure: Plant flower and/or vegetable seeds outside. Water them and discuss the fact that plants need soil, water and sunshine to grow.

- Discuss Activities of the Day

- Prepare to Leave / Dismissal

DAILY LESSON PLAN 65

Theme: Music

- Free Play

Special Activity A: "Book of Feelings"—"Love"
[See Table of Contents.]

Lesson Skill 31: Language Development

Objective: To increase listening comprehension by distinguishing louder and softer sounds

Materials: A bell

Procedure: Working with each child individually, have him/her listen while you ring the bell two times. Ask the child to tell if the first ring or the second ring was louder. Then ring twice again, and ask which ring was softer. Work with the child until he/she can easily hear the difference. Then have him/her ring the bell, louder and softer, telling which ring is which.

Lesson Skill 84c: Fine Motor Coordination

Objective: To improve small muscle abilities by putting puzzles together

Materials: Puzzles

Procedure: Have a group of four to six children work on individual puzzles. As each child finishes putting a puzzle together, count its pieces with him/her. Replace that puzzle with one having more pieces. Continue increasing the puzzles' difficulty until the child has trouble assembling it. Then help him/her to complete it. Note and record the number of pieces in the last puzzle completed independently.

- Handwork: Shakers

Materials: 8 oz. margarine tubs with lids, popcorn (unpopped), glue, craft sticks, felt markers.

Procedure: Have the children place about 10 kernels of popcorn in their margarine tubs. Then have them spread glue around the cover's edges and attach them to the tubs. Next, have them glue craft sticks to the tub bottoms. Also, after the glue dries, have them test their shakers by shaking them. Finally, have them decorate their shakers with felt markers.

- Clean Up

- Pre-Story Activities: Weather, Days of Week, Songs, Fingerplays, Sharing Time

Special Activity B: Musical Instruments

Procedure:

a) Play a tape or record featuring the music of an individual instrument. Show a picture of the instrument (or the actual instrument. Also, if possible, allow the children to carefully play the instrument.)

b) Invite parents, music teachers or others in the community to come in to play instruments or to sing for the children.

c) Have the children shake their shakers in time to various music tempos.

- Story

- Dismiss Group Procedure: Dismiss the children as they see their names on paper guitars. Read the names aloud for the children who do not recognize them.

- Snack

- Science Experience

- Outside Activities and/or Games

Special Activity C: Symphonic Music

Procedure: Play symphonic music for the children to experience.

- Discuss Activities of the Day

- Prepare to Leave / Dismissal

DAILY LESSON PLAN 66

Theme: Music

- Free Play

Special Activity A: "Book of Feelings" — "Angry" [See Table of Contents.]

Lesson Skill 32: Language Development

Objective: To increase listening comprehension through xylophone patterns

Materials: Xylophone, hammer or stick

Procedure: Work with the children individually. Ask them to copy the tapping patterns that you make. Start with two taps, in a 1-2 pattern. Then go on to three taps, in a 1-2-3 pattern. Next, have the children make some tapping patterns for the Teacher to copy. Also, go on to 4 and 5 tap patterns if the children are ready.

Lesson Skill 47c: Memory

Objective: To recall data necessary to name the days of the week

Procedure: Working with each child individually, ask him/her to name the days of the week. Record the responses in terms of the order in which they are given and the completeness of the list.

- **Handwork: Sandpaper Rhythm Blocks**

Materials: Pieces of wood (1" x 3" x 6", 2 per child), sandpaper (6" x 4 1/2"), tacks, hammer, felt markers

Procedure: Have the children use the hammer to tack the sandpaper to the sides of the wood. Then have them decorate the wooden backs with felt markers. Show the children how to rub the sandpaper blocks together to make rhythmic sounds to go with music.

- Clean Up

- Pre-Story Activities: Weather, Days of Week, Songs, Fingerplays, Sharing Time

Special Activity B: Musical Instruments

Procedure:

a) Play a tape or record featuring the music of an individual instrument. Show a picture of the instrument (or the actual instrument). Also, if possible, allow the children to carefully play the instrument.

b) Invite parents, music teachers or others in the community to come in to play instruments or to sing for the children.

c) Have the children use their sand blocks to keep time to various music tempos.

- Story

- Dismiss Group Procedure: Cut out construction paper bells of all colors. Dismiss the children as they recognize the color on their clothing as the colors of the bells.

- Snack

- Science Experience

- Outside Activities and/or Games

Special Activity C: Opera

Procedure: Play opera music for the children to experience.

- Discuss Activities of the Day

- Prepare to Leave / Dismissal

DAILY LESSON PLAN 67

Theme: Music

- Free Play

Special Activity A: "Book of Feelings"—"Compilation" [See Table of Contents.]

Special Activity B: Height/Weight Charts [See Table of Contents]

  Procedure: Record the children's heights on height chart. Compare them to their heights at the beginning of the year. Also, record their weights and the date on their anecdotal records.

Lesson Skill 90: Visual Motor Coordination

  Objective: To develop eye-hand coordination by completing special designs

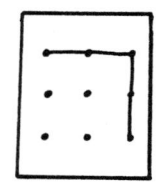

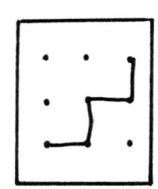

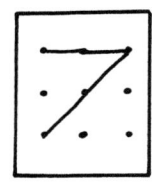

  Materials: Lesson sheets, pencil

  Procedure: Give the children sheets with designs on them (one by one). Give them another sheet with only dots on it. Have the children copy the designs given by connecting the dots.

Lesson Skill 46: Memory

  Objective: To recall data necessary to tell activities of preschool day

  Materials: Sequence of Day cards (Use only if necessary.)

  Procedure: Working with each child individually, ask him/her to tell the sequence of the school day, starting with free play and continuing on through the day. (For those children who can't recall activities, use the Sequence of Day cards as a prompt.)

- Handwork: Drums

  Materials: Coffee cans with plastic lids, drill, rope, dowel (16" or longer, 1/4" diameter), saw, clamp

  Procedure: Help each child to drill two holes (one across from the other) about 1/2 inch from the top of the can. Then have the child thread one end of the rope through a hole and tie it; thread the other end through the other hole and tie it. The rope forms a strap long enough for the child to slip the strap over his/her head and hold the drum while it is being played. Next, help the children clamp and saw the dowel into two pieces (drum sticks) at least 8" long.

- Clean Up

- Pre-Story Activities: Weather, Days of Week, Songs, Fingerplays, Sharing Time

Special Activity C: Single Instrument

  Procedure: Play music featuring an individual instrument from a tape or record. Show a picture of the instrument (or show the actual instrument, if possible, and allow the children to carefully play it.)

- Story

- Dismiss Group Procedure: Dismiss the children as they recognize their ages as you write them on a drum which is drawn on the chalkboard.

- Snack

- Science Experience

- Outside Activities and/or Games

  Procedure: Play marching music outside. Encourage interested children to march and pretend to be playing instruments in a band.

- Discuss Activities of the Day

- Prepare to Leave / Dismissal

3

CURRICULUM AIDS

The Daily Lesson Plans frequently call for the use of one or more of the following charts and lesson cards.

A. ALPHABET TRAIN

Procedure: Make an engine, 26 cars, and a caboose. Place the train on a wall where the children can see it easily. Each day, have a different child choose a picture showing an object, the name of which starts with that day's letter. Begin with the letter "A." Have the child name the object in the picture. Have the class repeat the name of the object, say the first letter of its name, pronounce the sound of that letter in the name, and say the whole name again. Tape the picture onto the "A" car. Continue in the same manner with letters "B" through "Z" on following days.

B. COLOR WHEEL

Procedure: Use the Color Wheel for identifying the colors that the children know and for teaching the names of colors that they do not know. To teach unfamiliar colors, point out objects and name their colors. Have the child say the color names, too, and then find other objects of the same color(s). Place the Color Wheel in the room where the children can use it in their free time.

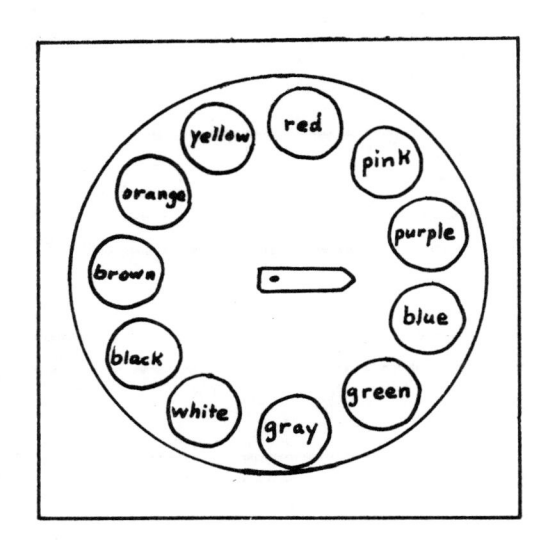

C. DAYS OF THE WEEK CHART

Procedure: Use this chart during the Pre-Story period every school day. Have the children take turns driving the car to the road sign for that day.

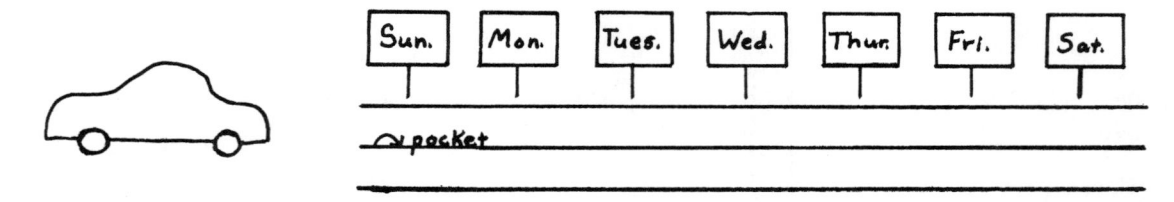

D. HEIGHT CHART

Procedure: Record the heights of the children (and the date when recorded) at the beginning, the middle, and the end of the school year. To make the chart, use paper 2' x 3" for each child in the class. Measure and mark inches on the left edge. Place the chart on a wall so that its bottom edge is 1 yard above the floor. Keep the chart on display all year for the children to observe.

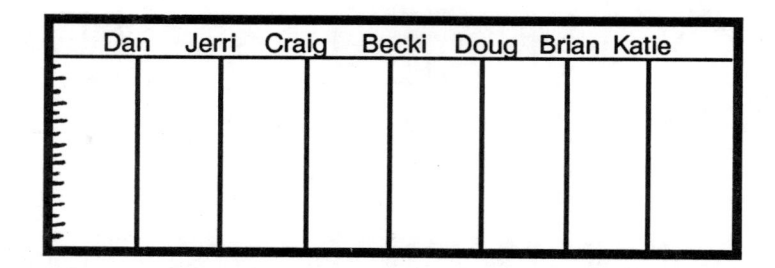

E. POCKET CHART

Procedure: To make a Pocket Chart, use a large piece of heavy paper such as paper tablecloth. Fold the paper into three horizontal pockets. Then staple or tape along its edges.

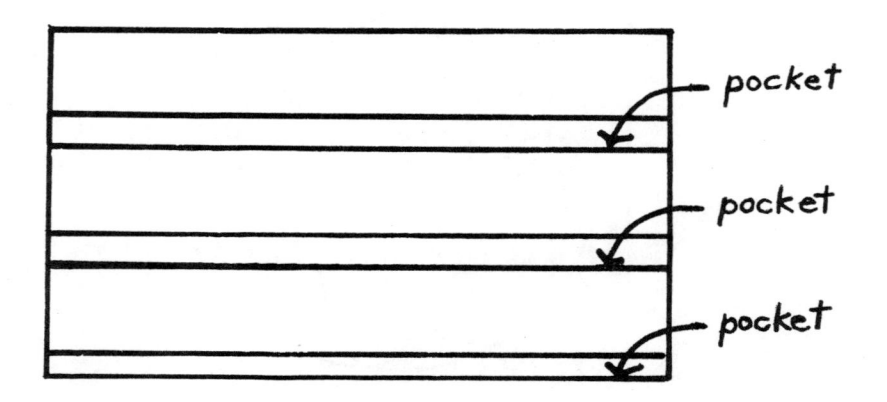

F. WEATHER CHART

Procedure: Draw and color the pictures on the Weather Chart. For durability, cover them with transparent adhesive film. Cut out a cardboard dial and attach it to the center of the chart with a brad.

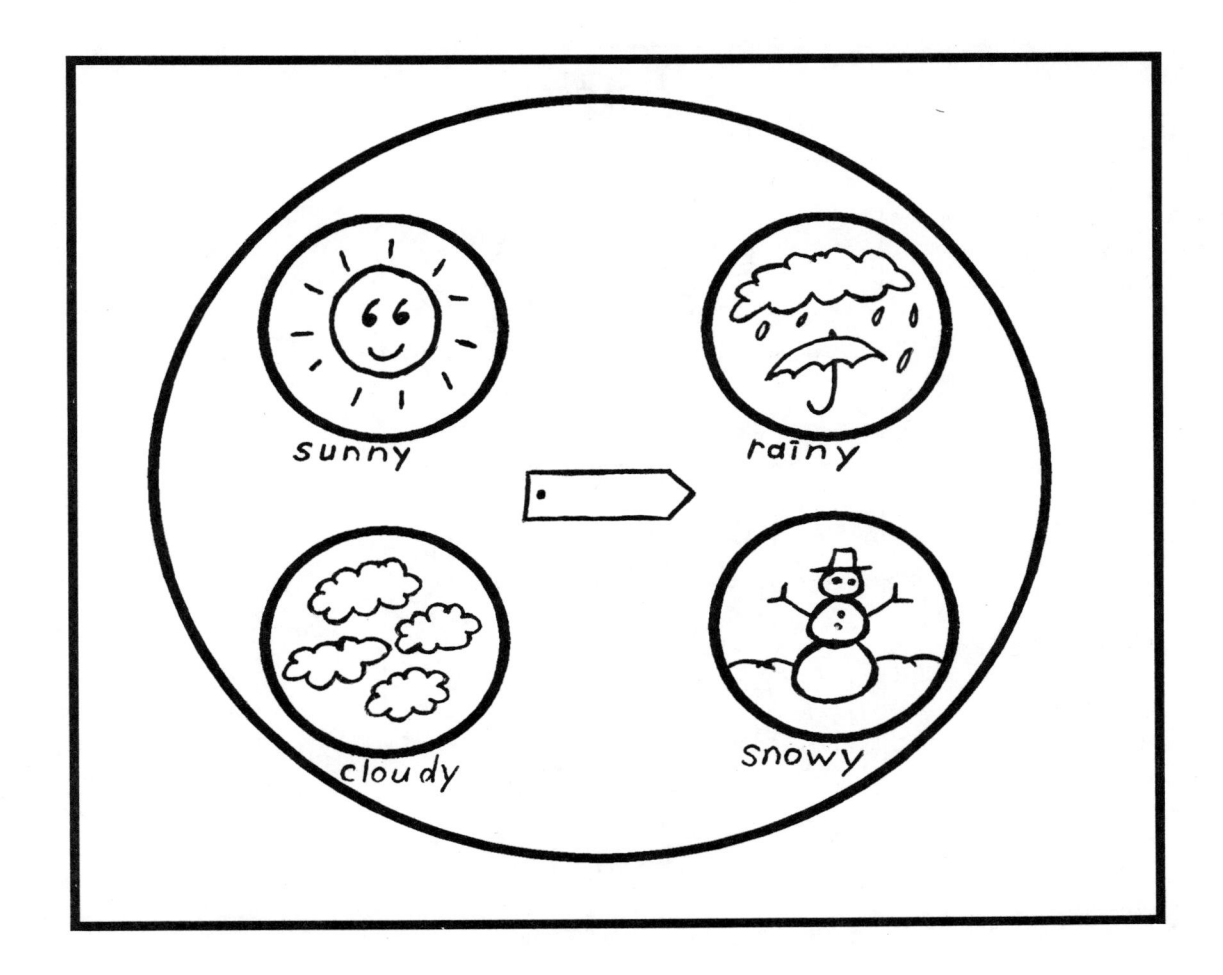

G. SEQUENCE OF DAY CARDS

Procedure: Enlarge these pictures, color them, and mount them on tagboard. For durability, cover them with transparent adhesive film. Display the cards at the appropriate times of the day to give children visual as well as verbal clues to let them know when it is time to change activities. Prominently display the cards in the pocket chart, on the ledge of the chalkboard or punch a hole in the top center of the cards and hang them on a hook.

Curriculum Aids

Sequence of Day Cards

- Story
- Snack
- Science Experience
- Outside

Sequence of Day Cards

Free Play

Lesson

Art

Clean Up

Curriculum Aids 89

H. INITIAL SOUND CARDS

Initial Sound Cards		
acorn	apron	airplane
ax	apple	ant
bell	book	banana
cactus	caterpillar	candle

Initial Sound Cards					
duck	doughnuts	door	gasoline	guitar	goat
eagle	eleven	ear	hat	heart	house
elephant	egg	elf	island	iron	ice cream
faucet	fire	fence	igloo	Indian	ink pen

Curriculum Aids 91

Initial Sound Cards					
jacks	jack-o-lantern	jump rope	net	nose	nest
kite	key	kitten	orange	opossum	overalls
leaf	lamp	lion	otter	octopus	ostrich
moon	mattress	mitten	pie	pear	pig

Initial Sound Cards

quilt	queen	quail	unicorn	ukelele	uniform
rose	rooster	rabbit	umbrella	undershirt	upstairs
seal	sun	sandbox	violin	vase	vacuum
tent	tiger	towel	windmill	watermelon	wand

Curriculum Aids

Initial Sound Cards		
yo-yo	yarn	yak
zebra	zipper	zero
chair	cherries	chick
wheel	whale	whistle

I. RHYMING WORD CARDS

Rhyming Word Cards		
moon	spoon	balloon
lock	sock	clock
fan	can	pan
key	tree	bee

Curriculum Aids

95

Rhyming Word Cards					
house	mouse	blouse	pie	eye	fly
pear	chair	bear	cake	rake	lake
dog	log	frog	stop	mop	top
car	star	jar	slip	ship	paperclip

Rhyming Word Cards					
train	plane	cane	rocket	pocket	locket
flag	bag	tag	pail	nail	sail
bread	bed	thread	jug	rug	lady bug
bone	phone	cone	cat	bat	hat

4

CURRICULUM ACTIVITY SELECTIONS

The resource activities and examples in this chapter have been proven to be suitable for use in preschool classrooms. Their order of presentation corresponds to their order in the Daily Lesson Plans.

A. FREE PLAY ACTIVITIES

Free play is the starting activity for every school day. The following examples offer a rich variety of learning experiences.

==
Free Play Activity Suggestions
==

[Photocopy these activities and mount them on index cards.]

Self-Awareness - Footprint Paths
Cut out many footprints. Make a path with them for the children to follow. Let the children make paths for others to follow. Have several sets of footprints, each a different color, so that different paths can be followed.

Self-Awareness - Felt Faces
From felt, cut heads and facial parts. Have the children arrange these on the felt board.

Self-Awareness - Drawing in Sand
Bring in a box with low sides containing about 1/4" layer of sand. Have the children draw faces and people. For reference, have a variety of face pictures near the box.

Fall - Applesauce
Make applesauce. Have the children remove the stems and wash the apples. Quarter the apples and put them unpeeled in a pan to cook. Cook the apples until they are soft, then run them through a food mill, having the children take turns turning the crank. Serve and enjoy.

Fall - Pumpkin Seed Toasting
Wash seeds and soak them in salty water overnight (1 tablespoon salt per 1 1/3 cups water). Then place the seeds on a cookie sheet and bake at 300 degrees for 20 minutes. Eat with or without shells.

Fall - Leaf Mobile
Have the children cut out leaves drawn on fall-colored construction paper. Tape string to leaves and tie strings to a branch.

Explorers - Columbus' Santa Maria
Get a large box from an appliance or furniture store. Make a boat from it, cutting it so the children can easily step into it. Have them paint it. Name it the Santa Maria. Place the box next to a wall where a sail can be displayed to look like it is attached to the boat. The children may pretend they are Columbus sailing across the Atlantic Ocean to America.

Shapes - Sewing Cards
Cut circle, square, rectangle, triangle, diamond and oval shapes from tagboard. Punch holes around the edges. Tie a piece of yarn to each card. Have enough sewing cards so that each child may choose one to take home. Discuss the shapes they choose and show them how to sew around the cards.

Shapes - Bean Bag Toss
Make bean bags in the shape of a circle, a triangle, and a square. Cut large shapes (a circle, a triangle and a square) from cardboard and color these to match the bean bags. Have the children toss the bean bags to the matching cardboard shapes.

Shapes - Collage
Have shapes (circles, ovals, squares, rectangles, triangles and diamonds) cut from fabric, construction paper and wallpaper available for the children to use in making collages.

Shapes - Sponge Paint
Cut 1" thick foam rubber or sponges into the shapes of diamonds and triangles. Have the children dip these shapes into shallow pans of paint and print them on paper.

Winter - Stringing Popcorn
Work with the children in small groups or individually as they will need help getting started. Caution them to be careful not to poke themselves with the needles. Popcorn slips easily on invisible thread. Place the strings of popcorn on trees, inside and outside. In a few days, check to see if the popcorn outside is being eaten by the birds.

Winter - Pine Needle Painting
The children paint white designs on green construction paper using pine needles.

Winter - Holiday Gift/Plaster Hand Print
Mix enough plaster for 2 or 3 hand prints at a time. Spread the plaster into a 5" or larger plastic lid. Each child makes an impression of his or her hand in the plaster. Scratch name and the date in the plaster hand print. Put the impressions in a place where they will not be accidentally broken while drying. Let them dry at least a week before removing them from the lids. Let them dry longer before the children wrap them.

Winter - Holiday Gift Wrapping Paper
Place drops of colored paint on plain white tissue paper. Have the children blow the paint with a straw to make designs. When dry, this wrapping paper may be used to wrap gifts such as the plaster hand prints for the parents.

Winter - White Paint on Dark Paper
Have the children paint with white paint on dark paper, making wintery scenes or other designs and pictures.

Senses - Slides of Faces
The children draw faces on slides with permanent felt markers. (Unwanted slides may be cleared for this use by wiping with chlorine bleach.) Show these slides sometime during the same day.

Senses - Taste
Bring in small cubes of fruit and vegetables. The children eat the cubes with toothpicks and tell what they are eating.

Senses - Magnification
Have the children look at each other with magnifying glasses, noticing ears, eyes, noses, mouths and hands.

Family - Houses
Have magazine pictures of furniture for every room in a house available for the children to glue on paper. They will make their own rooms and arrangements.

Valentine's Day - Stamping Valentines

Have a heart shaped stamp set available for the children to apply as "post marks" on their Valentine envelopes.

Valentine's Day - Crayon Rub Over Hearts

Under white paper, place hearts of various sizes cuts from construction paper. Rub red crayon over the white paper to reveal impressions of the heart shapes.

Patriotic Holidays - Currency and Coins

Place 100 pennies and a dollar bill on a table for the children to observe. Let them build with, count or otherwise manipulate the pennies. Explain that 100 pennies will buy the same thing that a dollar will buy. Talk about the pictures on the money. Explain who and what they picture.

Transportation - Transportation Slides

Have the children draw vehicles on slides with permanent felt markers. (Unwanted slides may be cleared for this use by wiping them with chlorine bleach.) Show these slides sometime the same day.

Health - Place Mats

The children finger paint on non-absorbent 12" x 18" paper. When the paint is dry, cover both sides with clear contact film. Overlap the edges, 1/2" on all sides.

Spring - Egg Carton Lily

Place a lily on a table. On the same table, place the cup portions cut from white egg cartons, green crayons, glue and large sheets of paper. Allow the children to decide what they will make with these materials, if anything.

Spring - Kite Decorating

Buy several kites that are plain. Have the children draw pictures or designs on them. Then assemble them and fly them during "Outside" time.

Day and Night - Sky Mobiles

All interested children cut out a sun, a cloud, a moon and a star. They punch a hole in each and tie them to a straw.

Farms - Stencils

Have shapes of farm objects available for the children to trace around.

Animals - Zoo Keeper's Hat

Have the children make zoo keepers' hats by gluing a 4" x 6" piece of construction paper with "Zoo Keeper" written on it to an 18" band of paper. Tape the band's ends together on each child's heads. While wearing these hats, have the children pretend to feed animals, clean cages, make soft beds of hay, etc.

Animals - Spider's Web

Have the children glue string on dark sheets of construction paper. They may make this into a spider's web or any other design. Show a real spider's web or a picture of one.

Animals - Caterpillars

Cut the bottom of an egg carton in half lengthwise to form 2 caterpillar bodies. Turn upside down and have the children paint the body and a face. They may also add pipe cleaners for antennae to complete their caterpillars.

Plants - Seed Planting

With potting soil, cups, seeds, water and spoons or other digging tools, help each child plant seeds of his or her own choosing. Have the children be responsible for watering the seeds when they are dry. Plants such as tomatoes may be transplanted (and later produce something to eat). Marigolds and other flowers are enjoyable.

Plants - Citrus Seeds

Cut an orange, a lemon and a grapefruit in half. Remove their seeds, plant them in soil in paper cups, and water them. Place a picture of the fruit the seed came from on each cup.

Plants - Grassy Sponge

Keep a sponge wet in a shallow pan of water. Sprinkle grass seed on the sponge and watch it grow.

Music - Music Writing

Have sheets of paper with five lines drawn on them. Show the children how to write musical notes (circles, circles with sticks, filled-in circles with sticks). They put these notes on or between the lines. Play the music they have written on any musical instrument that you have.

Music - Collage of Musical Instruments

Cut out pictures of musical instruments from catalogs or magazines. Talk about the instruments. Have the children glue these on paper (one large sheet on which they may work together, or small sheets for individuals.)

Music - Director's Wand

Use pieces of dowel or strips of heavy cardboard about 12" long. Have the children paint them and tape 2 inches of foil around each end. Play music for them to direct.

Music - Water Glasses

Use water glasses of the same size. Vary the water level in each glass. Have the children tap them with a spoon and listen to the different pitches.

Music - Drawing to Music

Have the children draw on paper with crayons, colored pencils and/or felt markers while listening to music. Play different types of music with varied rhythms during this time.

Miscellaneous - String Art

Have the children place pieces of string or yarn of all colors in glue and then lay them on paper, making designs.

Miscellaneous - Sawdust Designs

Have the children spread glue on dark paper. Then have them sprinkle sawdust on the glue. Shake excess off.

Miscellaneous - Stringing Along

Have the children string styrofoam beads, macaroni, or empty spools of thread.

1. **SPECIAL FREE PLAY ACTIVITIES**

    a. **Alphabet Book**

Description: Consisting of 26 pages, the Alphabet Book helps the children to perceive the relationship between letters of the alphabet and specific words that start with the letters.

Procedure: Each child glues a pre-cut letter "A" on 8 1/2" x 11" paper. Then, he or she chooses a picture of an object from the group whose name starts with this letter and glues it on the same page. The teacher writes the name of the object on the paper. Have the children do the same for letters "B" through "Z."

    b. **Book of Colors**

Description: Consisting of 11 pages for each of 11 different colors, the Book of Colors provides children with opportunities to match the names of colors with objects that are those colors.

Procedure: Have each child glue green leaves onto a tree drawn on 5 1/2" x 8 1/2" sheet of paper. Write "Green" at the bottom of the paper.

Make pages for other colors using pictures of:

blue birds	white snowmen	yellow suns	purple grapes	red hearts
gray keys	black kittens	brown dogs	orange oranges	pink flowers

c. Numeral Book of Tiny Things

Description: Consisting of 10 pages, the Numeral Book gives children the opportunity to match numerals to values.

Procedure: Have each child glue one toothpick on 5 1/2" x 8 1/2" paper. Write the numeral and the name of the object at the bottom of the page.

Do the same with the following items:

2 buttons	4 paper clips	6 stick-on stars	8 beads	10 marigold seeds
3 washers	5 rubber bands	7 sequins	9 pieces of rice	

d. Book of Feelings

Description: Consisting of 12 pages, the Book of Feelings allows children the opportunity to recognize and compare the characteristics of various feelings.

Procedure: On 5 1/2" x 8 1/2" paper, write the words "I feel happy when_____." Have the children complete the sentence. Then have them draw pictures on their pages to illustrate the feeling.

Make pages for each of the feelings:

sad	brave	bored	love	sorry	afraid
proud	hurt	safe	angry	excited	

===
* Book Compilation—procedure for all books—have all the children meet in a group. Explain that today they will take their books home. First though, they must arrange the pages in order. Hand out pages in reverse order. Have children stack the pages face up. Then hand out covers and staple the pages in place.
===

B. SONGS

There are many delightful songs suitable for preschool singers to learn and enjoy. The following song books offer many from which to choose.

1) *Do Your Ears Hang Low* by Tom Glazer, illustrated by Mila Lazarevich. Doubleday & Company, Inc., Garden City, New York, 1980

2) *Eye Winker Tom Tinker Chin Chopper* by Tom Glazer, illustrated by Ron Himler. A Zephyr Book, Doubleday & Company, Inc., Garden City, New York, 1973.

3) *Holiday Song Book* selections, illustrations & additional lyrics by Robert Quackenbush. All music arranged for easy piano & guitar by Harry Bush. Lothrop, Lee & Shepard Co., A Division of William Morrow & Co., Inc., 150 Madison Ave., New York, New York 10016, 1977.

4) *190 Children's Songs* compiled & edited by David Nelson. Robbins Music Corp., NY, NY, 1967.

Among the many well-known songs in these books, the following selections are especially recommended. They are arranged and labeled by categories to indicate their relationship to particular Lesson Themes. Also, they are coded: 1), 2), 3) or 4), to indicate in which of the above books they may be found.

SELF-AWARENESS

1) "Head, Shoulders, Knees and Toes"
1) "I Point to Myself"
2) "Put Your Finger in the Air"

EXPLORERS

3) "He Knew the Earth Was Round"

HOLIDAYS

1) "Jingle Bells"
3) "Hanukkah Song"
3) "My Dreydel"
3) "The Twelve Days of Christmas"
3) "Lincoln and Liberty"
3) "Washington the Great"
4) "Jolly Old St. Nicholas"
4) "Deck the Halls"

SENSES

1) "Do Your Ears Hang Low"

FAMILY

4) "Over the River and Through the Woods"

VALENTINE'S DAY

3) "Mister Frog Went a-Courting"
3) "A Paper of Pins"
3) "Billy Boy"

TRANSPORTATION

2) "Bus Song"

DAY AND NIGHT

4) "Twinkle, Twinkle, Little Star"
4) "Lazy Mary Will You Get Up"

FARM

4) "Farmer in the Dell"
4) "Baa Baa Black Sheep"
4) "Mairzy Doats"
2) "Old MacDonald"

ANIMALS

2) "Eensy Weensy Spider"
2) "Little White Duck"
2) "Bear Went Over the Mountain"
2) "I Know an Old Lady"

SPECIAL FAMILY DAYS

3) "Mama's Gonna Buy"

PLANTS

2) "The Mulberry Bush"
4) "Mistress Mary Quite Contrary"

GENERAL

1) "Here We Go Looby Loo"
1) "The Hokey Pokey"
1) "If You're Happy"
2) "Peter Hammers"
2) "I'm A Little Teapot"
2) "The More We Are Together"
2) "This Old Man"
4) "The A B C Song"

C. FINGERPLAYS

Fingerplays introduce children to poetry and encourage self-expression. The children vocalize words and move their bodies allowing the meaning of the words to be absorbed. They also help children "get their wiggles out," so that they can settle down for a quiet activity such as listening to a story. Most importantly, they are fun.

[Note: Fingerplays are organized by themes to correspond with those in the daily lesson plans. Photocopy these activities and glue them onto file cards. Label each card according to its theme. Paper clip daily selections to lesson plans.]

SELF-AWARENESS

I'll touch my hair, my lips, my eyes
I'll sit up straight and then I'll rise
I'll touch my ears, my nose, my chin
Then quietly sit down again.
*

My hands upon my head I'll place
Upon my shoulders, upon my face
At my knees and by my side
And then behind me they will hide.
Then I'll raise them way up high
And let my fingers fly, fly, fly.
Then I'll clap them 1, 2, 3
See how quiet they can be.
*

Open them, shut them
Let your hands go clap.
Open them, shut them
Lay them in your lap.
Walk them, walk them
Right up to your chin.
Open up your little mouth
But do not let them in.
I have ten little fingers (Hold both hands up.)
And they all belong to me. (Point to self.)
I can make them do things.
Would you like to see?
I can open them up wide.
I can shut them up tight.
I can put them together.
I can put them out of sight.
I can raise them up high.
I can bring them down low.
I can fold them together.
And keep them just so.
*

I wiggle my fingers
I wiggle my toes
I wiggle my shoulders
I wiggle my nose
Now all the wiggles are out of me
So I can sit as still as can be.
*

Touch your forehead and your chin
That's the way the game begins.
Touch your hair and then your ear
Now touch your lower lip right here.
Touch your eye and then your knees
(Now pretend you're going to sneeze.)
Touch your elbow where it bends
That's the way the touch game ends.
*

I'll touch my chin, my cheek, my chair
I'll touch my head, my heels, my hair
I'll touch my knees, my neck, my nose
I'll dip way down and touch my toes
*

FALL

Way up high in an apple tree
(Point up.)
Two round red apples smiled at me
(Make apples with thumbs and forefingers.)
I shook that tree as hard as I could
(Make shaking motion with hands.)
Down fell the apples
(Lower hands.)
Mmmmm! Were they good! (Rub tummy.)
*

The little leaves are falling down
(Wiggle fingers from above head to floor.)
Round and round and round.
(Stand and turn around.)
The little leaves are falling down
(Wiggle fingers from above head to floor.)
Falling to the ground.
(Sit on floor.)
Scarecrow, scarecrow turn around
Scarecrow, scarecrow jump up and down
Scarecrow, scarecrow arms up high
Scarecrow, scarecrow wink an eye
Scarecrow, scarecrow bend your knees
Scarecrow, scarecrow flop in the breeze
Scarecrow, scarecrow climb in bed
Scarecrow, scarecrow rest your head.

*

Here's a wide-eyed owl
(Make two circles with thumbs and forefingers and place circles in front of eyes.)
With a pointed nose.
(Point forefingers together in front of nose.)
Two pointed ears
(forefingers pointing up by each ear)
And claws for toes
(fingers spread out in front of feet)
He lives high up in a tree
(Point up.)
And when he looks at you
(Hold hand in position of shading eyes.)
He flaps his wings.
(Wave hands at sides.)
And says, "Whoo! Whoo!"
(Cup mouth with hands.)

*

Here's a leaf all yellow and brown.
(Hold out one hand.)
Here's a leaf that Johnny found.
(Hold out other hand—may say any child's name.)
Put them together and you will have two
One for me and one for you.
(Point to self and then someone else.)

*

SHAPES

Draw a circle, draw a circle
Round as can be.
Draw a circle, draw a circle
Just for me.
Draw an oval, draw an oval
Shaped like an egg
Draw an oval, draw an oval
Now with your leg.
Draw a rectangle, draw a rectangle
Shaped like a door
Draw a rectangle, draw a rectangle
With corners four.
Draw a triangle, draw a triangle
With corners three
Draw a triangle, draw a triangle
Just for me.
Draw a diamond, draw a diamond
Shaped like a kite
Draw a diamond, draw a diamond
With all your might.
(Draw shapes in air with hand.)

*

HOLIDAYS

The turkey is a funny bird
His head goes wobble, wobble
(Wobble head.)
And all he says is just one word,
Gobble, gobble, gobble.

Here is a turkey
With his tail spread wide.
(Make turkey with hand and spread fingers.)
He sees the farmer coming
And he tries to hide.
(Cover with other hand.)
He runs across the barnyard
Wobble, wobble, wobble
(Move hand from one side of body to the other.)
Talking turkey talk
Gobble, gobble, gobble.
(Wiggle thumb.)

*

Wake up little Pilgrims
(Open eyes wide.)
The sun is in the East
(Join hands above head to make sun.)
Today is the day for our Thanksgiving feast.
Come, jump out of bed
(Jump up.)
See how tall you can stand
(Stand tall.)
My, my! You're a wide awake band
Wash your hands, wash your faces
(Act out washing.)
So that you will look neat
Then come to the table so we may eat
(Act out eating.)
*

Here is Santa's workshop
(Hold forefingers together.)
Here is Santa Claus
(Hold up thumb.)
Here are Santa's little elves
(Hold up four fingers.)
Putting toys upon the shelves
(Pantomime)
Back and forth they scamper
Busy as can be
(Move fingers back and forth.)
Now they help to chop and trim
Santa's Christmas tree
(Pantomime)
*

Santa Claus is big and fat
(Join hands out from stomach.)
He wears black boots
(Touch feet.)
And a bright red hat
(Touch nose.)
Just like a rose
And he Ho-ho-hos
From his head to his toes.
(Touch head and toes.)
*

We'll hang up our stockings   (Pantomime)
And when we're asleep
(Rest head on hands.)
Down into our house old Santa will creep.
(Tiptoe about.)
He'll fill all our stockings
with presents and then   (Pantomime)
Santa and his reindeer will scamper again.
(Wiggle fingers while moving hand in air.)
So clap, clap your hands
And sign out with glee
For Christmas is coming
And merry are we. (Smile)
*

A present is a funny thing
(Show gift-wrapped box.)
It always sets me wondering.
(Finger by side of head.)
For whether it is thin or wide
(Hold hands close together and then far apart.)
You never know just what's inside.
*

Five little bunnies sitting near a tree.
The first one said,
"The Easter bunny's me."
The second one said,
"I've a hat on my head."
The third one said,
"I'll paint the egg red."
The fourth one said,
"That will never do.
Everyone knows Easter eggs are blue."
The fifth one said,
"Let's not quarrel today.
Let's hop and hop and hop away."
(Have five children pretend to be bunnies
and stand in front of the group. Touch
each bunny's shoulders as you say his/her
line. They all hop away at the end.)
*

WINTER

Thumbs in thumb place
(Hold up hand and wiggle thumb.)
Fingers all together (fingers together)
This is the song we sing
In mitten weather.
*

Little Jack Frost pinched my nose.
Little Jack Frost pinched my nose.
But I ran into the house and shut the door
So he couldn't pinch me anymore.
*

Warm hands warm. Do you know how?
If you want to warm your hands
Do what I do now.
(Say above before each action such as rubbing
them together sitting on them, blowing on them,
putting them in your pockets, putting mittens on.)
*

I'm going to build a little house
(Join forefingers together to make a house.)
With windows big and bright
(Draw window with finger.)
With chimney tall and curling smoke
(Hold a finger on the chimney finger
and move it away like curling smoke.)
Drifting out of sight.
(Hold a finger on chimney finger and
move it away like curling smoke.)
In winter when the snowflakes fall
(Wiggle fingers from above head down to floor.)
Or when I hear a storm (Hold hand to ear.)
I'll go inside my little house
Where I'll be safe and warm. (Hug self with arms.)
*

Five little icicles hanging in a row
The first one said, "It's cold, you know."
The second one said, "We're shining bright."
The third one said, "We're a beautiful sight."
The fourth one said, "Look up there!"
The fifth one said, "Where, Where?"
It was the sun. It melted the snow.
The five little icicles said, "Here we go!"
(Hold fingers downward to represent icicles—
fold them up on the last line.)
*

"Winter" says Grandma, "Is hard
when you're old. Pile on blankets.
My, but it's cold."
"Winter," say the children, "Is perfect
for me. Snowballs and snowmen and
sledding–Wheeee!"
(pantomime action)
"Winter," says Father, "Means
shoveling snow and slipping on
ice while biting winds blow."
"Winter," says Mother, "Means
mittens are lost. And noses are
nipped in shivery frost."
*

I'm big and round at the bottom.
(Bend down joining hands to make a circle.)
I'm small and round at the top.
(Hands form a circle around face.)
And in the middle I'm middle-sized
(Shape arms in circle by middle.)
And I carry a broom or a mop.
(Pretend to hold a broom.)
I stand up straight on each frosty day
(Stand straight.)
But when it's warm I melt away.
(Slowly crumble to the floor.)
What am I? (snow person)
*

JOBS

Ten brave firemen sleeping in a row.
(Lay ten fingers in your lap.)
Ding goes the bell, down the pole they go.
(Act out sliding down pole)
Jumping on the engine, Oh! Oh! (Jump)
Putting out the fire,
(Spray with hose.)
Back home so slow.
(Walk about slowly.)
Back to bed again, all in a row.
(Lay fingers in lap again.)
*

Who says "stop"? The traffic cop.
(Hold hand out.)
Listen to the whistle blow; toot, toot, toot.
(Pretend to blow whistle.)
Who says "go" in the rain and snow?
(Motion for cars to go.)
Listen to the whistle blow; toot, toot, toot.
(Pretend to blow whistle.)
*

The carpenter's hammer goes tap, tap, tap.
And his saw goes see, saw, see.
He planes and he measures
And he saws and he hammers
While he builds a house for me.
*

SENSES

When I close my eyes, what do I see?
(Touch eyes.)
I see a flower and maybe a tree.
When I close my eyes, what do I hear?
(Touch ears.)
Soft sounds, loud sounds, far and near.
When I close my eyes, what do I taste?
(Touch mouth.)
Striped stick candy and white toothpaste.
When I close my eyes, what do I smell?
(Touch nose.)
Strawberry ice cream and brown caramel.
When I close my eyes, what do I touch?
(Hold out hands.)
My kitty's soft fur that I like so much.
*

VALENTINE'S DAY

The first little valentine
Had a funny face.
The second little valentine
Was all made of lace.
The third little valentine's hearts
Numbered two.
The fourth little valentine
Said, "I love you."
The fifth little valentine
Said, "I love you, too."
(Make a valentine for each line as described.)
*

Five gay Valentine's from the 10 cent store,
I sent one to Mother, now there are four.
Four gay Valentines, pretty ones to see.
I gave one to Brother, now there are three.
Three gay Valentines, yellow, red and blue.
I gave one to sister, now there are two.
Two gay Valentines, my we have fun.
I gave one to Daddy, now there is one.
One gay Valentine, the story is almost done
I gave it to Baby, now there are none.
(Hold up five Valentines, taking away one at
a time as indicated.)
*

I made a snowman yesterday
So jolly, fat and fine.
(Join hands in front of stomach and smile.)
I pinned a red heart on his chest
And named him "Valentine."
(Form heart shape with fingers.)
*

TRANSPORTATION

Red light, stop
Yellow light, no
Wait for the green light
And then you may go.
(Show circles of each color at the
appropriate time or make a traffic
light and point to each color.)
*

Stop, look and listen
Before you cross the street.
Use your eyes, use your ears,
And then you use your feet.
(Point to eyes, ears, and feet
where indicated.)
*

Car, car, may I have a ride?
Yes sir, yes sir, step inside.
(Shake head "yes".)
Turn on the key.
Put your foot on the gas.
Now chug away, chug away.
But don't go too fast.
*

Here is a little train
Running up the track
It says, "toot - toot!"
And runs right back.
(Run fingers up and down arm.)
*

HEALTH

I wash my hands like this.
I wash my hands like this.
Every day before I eat
I wash my hands like this.
*

Our toothbrushes hang
In a neat little line.
We can tell one from another.
The blue one is Dad's
The red one is mine
And the green one
Belongs to my mother.
(Show real or paper toothbrushes of these colors.)
*

SPRING

It rained on Ann, it rained on Dan
It rained on Arabella.
It didn't rain on Mary Jane
She had an umbrella.
(Substitute names of children in your
group for all the names except Arabella.)
*

A little rain
(Wiggle fingers from above head to the floor.)
A little sun (Make an arc above head with arms.)
Out comes the blossoms
(Put hands together then spread apart.)
One by one.
*

Two little bunnies hopped down the lane   (Hop)
Under an umbrella to keep off the rain.
(Pretend to hold umbrella.)
They hopped and they played
Until the rain was over. (Hop)
Then they ran to the meadow
To nibble on some clover. (Nibble)
*

Pitter patter, pitter patter
Hear the raindrops say,
(Wiggle fingers from above head to floor.)
If a sunbeam should peek out
They'll be a rainbow gay.
(Make arc above head with hands joined.)
*

FARM

In the barnyard everyone will say
"Thank you for my food today."
The cow says, "Moo!"
The dog says, "Bow wow!"
The cat says "Mew mew"
The lamb says "Baa baa!"
The hen says, "Cluck cluck cluck!"
The horse says, "Hee, hee, hee!"
The pig says, "Oink, oink!"
The farmer thanks his animals every one
For the work that had been done.
(Children make animal sounds.)
*

Five little farmers
Woke up with the sun.
It was early morning
The chores must be done.
The first little farmer
Went to milk the cow.
The second little farmer
Thought he'd better plow.
The third little farmer
Fed the hungry hens.
The fourth little farmer
Mended broken pens.
The fifth little farmer
Took his vegetables to town.
When the work was finished
And the western sky was red.
Five little farmers tumbled into bed.
(Five children stand in front
of the group. Group does action
as each farmer does his or hers.)
*

ANIMALS

Mr. Rabbit has a habit
That is very cute to see.
He wrinkles up and crinkles up
His little nose at me.
(Wrinkle nose.)
I like my little rabbit
And I like his little brother
And we have a lot of fun
Making faces at each other.
*

I saw a little rabbit
That went hop, hop, hop. (Hop)
And he had big ears
That went flop, flop, flop.
(Raise arms by ears and flop them.)
*

I think when a little chicken drinks
He takes the water in his bill.
And then he holds his head way up
So the water can run downhill.
(Pantomime)
*

The little gray pony looked out of the barn.
He wants to go out to play!
The little gray pony jumps over the fence.
And gallops and gallops away.
He gallops and gallops away.
He gallops and gallops away.
The little gray pony jumped over the fence
And galloped and galloped away.
(Good for outside where children
can gallop as they wish.)
*

A little frog by a pond am I
Hippety, hippety, hop.
I can jump in the air so high
Hippety, hippety, hop. (Hop)
*

A wise old owl
Sat in an oak.
The more he saw
(Touch eyes.)
The less he spoke.
(Touch mouth.)
The less he spoke
(Touch mouth.)
The more he heard.
(Touch ear.)
Why can't you and I
(Point to a person and then self.)
Be like that wise old bird?
(Flap hands like wings.)
*

Two little monkeys jumping on the bed. (Jump)
One fell down and hurt his head.
(Hold hands to head.)
The other called the doctor
(Pretend to hold phone.)
And the doctor said,
"That's what you get for
jumping on the bed."
*

Frogs jump, caterpillars hump
Snakes slide, sea gulls glide
Worms wiggle, bugs jiggle
Mice creep, deer leap
Rabbits hop, horses clop
Puppies bounce, kittens pounce
Lions stalk, but I walk.
*

One, one; the zoo is lots of fun
Two, two; see a kangaroo.
Three, three; see a chimpanzee.
Four, four; hear the lions roar.
(Cup one hand over the other.)
Five, five; watch the seals dive.
Six, six; there's a monkey doing tricks.
Seven, seven; elephants eleven.
Eight, eight; a tiger and his mate.
Nine, nine; penguins in a line.
Ten, ten; I want to come again.
(Raise one finger for each line.)
Here is my turtle, he lives in a shell.
He likes his home so very well.
He sticks out his head when he wants to eat
(Poke thumb out from under cupped hand)
And he tucks it back in when he went to sleep.
(Draw thumb back in.)

*

Two little dickie birds
Sitting on the fence
One named _____, one named _____
Fly away _____, fly away _____
Come back _____, come back _____
(Use names of children in group.
Children flap arm and leave
group and them come back.)

*

Five little froggies sat on the shore.
One went for a swim
And then there were four.
Four little froggies looked out to sea.
One went swimming
And then there were three.
Three little froggies said,
"What can we do?"
One jumped into the water
And then there were two.
Two little froggies sat in the sun
One swam off
And then there was one.
One lonely froggy said,
"This is no fun."
He dived into the water
And then there was none.
(Use frogs on pocket chart taking
them down one at a time as indicated.)

*

This is the way the elephant goes
With curly trunk instead of a nose.
(arms hanging down with hands clasped,
body bent)
The buffalo all shaggy and fat
Has two sharp horns instead of a hat.
(forefingers placed on sides of head)
The hippo with his mouth so wide
Lets you see what's inside.
(Open mouth wide.)
The wiggly snake upon the ground
Crawls along without a sound.
(Move hand along like a snake.)
But monkey see and monkey do
Are the funniest animals in the zoo?
(Act like a monkey.)

*

We'll hop, hop, hop like a bunny
And run, run, run like a dog.
We'll walk, walk, walk like an elephant
And jump, jump, jump like a frog.
We'll swim, swim, swim like a goldfish
And fly, fly, fly like a bird.
We'll sit right down and fold our hands
And not say a single word.

*

I have five pets (Show five fingers.)
That I'd like you to meet,
They all live on Mulberry Street
This is my chicken, the smallest of all.
(Cup hands.)
He comes running whenever I call
(Walk two fingers.)
Hear my duck say, "Quack, quack, quack."
As he shakes the water from his back
(Shake body.)
Here is my rabbit, he hops from pen
(Hop in place.)
Then I must put him back again.
(Pretend to lift rabbit into pen.)
Here is my kitten, (Pet kitten in arm.)
Her coat is black and white.
She loves to sleep on my pillow at night
(Rest head on hands.)
Here is my puppy who has lots of fun.
He chases the others and makes them run.
(Run in place.)

*

There was a little turtle
He lived in a box
He swam in a puddle
He climbed on the rocks.
He snapped at a mosquito
He snapped at a flea.
He snapped at a minnow.
He snapped at me.
He caught the mosquito.
He caught the flea.
He caught the minnow.
But he didn't catch me.
(For snapping and catching, clap
hands with wrists together.)
*

PLANTS

Here is my garden
(Point to spot.)
I'll rake it with care   (Rake)
And them some seeds I'll plant in there.
(Plant seeds.)
The sun will shine
(Clasp hands in arc over head.)
The rain will fall
(Wiggle fingers from above head to the floor.)
And my garden will grow straight and tall.
(Stand straight.)
*

Whoopsie Daisy picked a daisy
On a summer day.
(Pretend to pick a daisy.)
Whoopsie Daisy picked a daisy
And then she ran away.
(Run in place.)
*

I dig, dig, dig and plant some seeds.
I rake, rake, rake and pull some weeds.
I wait and watch and soon I see
My garden growing up to my knee.
*

FAMILY

I help my family
I sweep the floor.
I dust the table
I run to the store.
I help beat eggs
And sift flour for cakes.
And we all eat
The good things we make.
*

This is my father (thumb)
This is my mother (index finger)
This is my brother (middle finger)
This is my sister (ring finger)
This is the baby (little finger)
Oh, how I love them.
*

I have a nice mother.
She's pretty and gay.
(Smile)
I love her so much.
I kissed her today.
(Throw kiss.)
*

The fish live in the little brook.
(Move hand like a fish.)
The birds live in the tree.
(Fly like bird.)
But home is the very nicest place.
For a little child like me.
*

BIRTHDAY

Today is _____'s birthday.
Let's make (him or her) a cake.
We'll mix and stir and mix and stir
Then into the oven bake.
Here's our cake so nice and round
We'll frost it pink and white.
_____candles on it we have found
To make (his or her) birthday bright.
*

GENERAL

Roll your arms so slowly
As slowly as slowly can be.
Roll your arms so slowly
And fold your arms like me.
Roll your arms so swiftly
As swiftly as swiftly can be.
Roll your arms so swiftly
And fold your arms like me.
Clap your hands so softly
As softly as softly can be.
Clap your hands so softly
And fold your hands like me.
Clap your hands so loudly
As loudly as loudly can be.
Clap your hands so loudly.
And fold your hands like me.
Go to sleep so lazy
As lazy as lazy can be.
Go to sleep so lazy
And close your eyes like me.
Wake up, wake up so brightly
As brightly as brightly can be.
Wake up, wake up so brightly
Sit up straight like me.

*

D. NUTRITIOUS SNACKS

Tasty and nutritious menus can be planned for most children by selecting from the wide variety of foods listed below. Be aware though, that some foods can cause allergic reactions in some children.

1. **Nutritious Food Selections**

   Beverages:

   - milk
   - fruit juices—apple, apricot, nectar, grapefruit, grape, orange, peach nectar, pear nectar, prune, pineapple, tangerine, tomato (also, fruit juice popsicles)

   Breads:

   - whole grain bread (regular or toasted), crackers, muffins, granola bars

   Protein:

   - cheese (slice, cube, spread), egg salad, deviled ham, chicken spread, tuna spread, deviled eggs, meat slices or wedges, peanut butter

   Fruits:

   - apples, raisins, bananas, oranges, pears, grapes, grapes (seedless), strawberries, blueberries, cherries, watermelon (seeds removed and cut into bite-size pieces), cantaloupe (cut into bite-size pieces), cherry tomatoes, apricots, dates, grapefruit sections, peaches, tangerine sections

   Vegetables:

   - broccoli, cabbage wedges, carrots, cauliflower, celery, cucumbers, green beans, green pepper, lettuce leaves, mushrooms, radishes, zucchini strips.

Curriculum Activity Selections

2. **Snack Menu Suggestions**

   a. Deviled ham on whole wheat bun, quartered–orange juice.
   b. Egg salad sandwiches, quartered–tangerine juice popsicles.
   c. Deviled eggs, whole wheat crackers–peach nectar.
   d. Tuna spread on whole wheat toast, quartered–pineapple juice.
   e. Chicken spread on whole wheat crackers–orange juice.
   f. Turkey slices (cut to fit) on whole wheat crackers–orange juice.
   g. Chicken spread on quartered whole wheat toast topped with grapes–apple juice.
   h. Peanut butter on apple slices–milk.
   i. Peanut butter on celery slices–apple juice.
   j. Peanut butter and grated carrots on whole wheat toast, quartered–tomato juice.
   k. Peanut butter and honey on whole wheat crackers–grapefruit juice.
   l. Peanut butter and raisins on snack crackers–grape juice.
   m. Peanut butter and banana slices on whole wheat crackers–pear nectar.
   n. Small boxes of raisins, whole wheat crackers–milk.
   o. Cored apples, toasted whole wheat bread, quartered–milk.
   p. Bananas, bran muffins–pineapple juice.
   q. Oranges, (seedless, peeled, sectioned), whole wheat crackers–milk.
   r. Strawberries, cream dip–milk.
   s. Cream cheese on snack crackers topped with cherries–milk.
   t. Fruit cups (blueberries, watermelon cubes without seeds, cantaloupe cubes)–milk.
   u. Bacon pieces sprinkled on cheese spread on whole wheat toast–tomato juice.
   v. Cauliflower, green beans, and green pepper dipped in melted cheese–pear nectar.
   w. Cheese kisses (individually wrapped balls of cheese), blueberries, whole wheat muffins–grape juice.
   x. Cheese melted on whole wheat toast cut in the shape of circles, squares, and triangles–apple juice.
   y. Cheese slices (individually wrapped), snack crackers–milk.

E. **SCIENCE EXPERIENCES**

Involving the children in a variety of simple, safe science "projects" is a good way to enhance the children's interest in their world. Set aside a table in the classroom and use it solely for the purpose of science experiences. Categories of the following science experiences include: Fall, Weather, Water, Stones, Air, Plants, Animals, Weight, Magnets, Shaker Container, Sniffing Bottles, Feel Box, and Chemicals. Many are related to themes presented in the Daily Lesson Plan and should be used accordingly.

===
Science Experiences
===

[Note: Choose daily science experiences in advance and note them on your plan. Also, transfer the science experiences to index cards.]

Fall - Fall Collection
Take the children on a nature hike. Collect all kinds of leaves, acorns, other nuts, pine needles, dried weeds, grass and whatever else interests the children. (Caution against poisonous choices.) Place these items on the science table to use in science experiences #2, 3, 4, and 5. Examine them with a magnifying glass.

Fall - Sort Fall Items
In boxes on the science table, place one of each type of item collected, except leaves. (Use them in the next experience.) Label each box. Have the children sort the rest by placing them in the correct boxes.

Fall - Sort Fall Leaves
In boxes on the science table, place one of each type of leaf collected. Label each box. Have the children sort the rest of the leaves by placing them in the correct boxes.

Fall - Water Play
Have the children find out which of the fall items collected float and which sink by placing them in a dishpan of water.

Fall - Weighing Fall Items
Using the collection of fall items, compare the weights of the various items by placing them on a balance scale.

Fall - Leaf Compression
Stuff a burlap bag or old pillow case with leaves. Tie end securely. Show the children how full it is. Have the children jump, roll, sit, hop, etc., on the bag or pillow case. Show that the bag or case is no longer full even though no leaves were taken out. Show that the leaves were pressed together and broken so they take up less room.

Weather - Weather Indicator
Sprinkle cobalt chloride on a cotton ball and place the cotton in on open glass container. The cotton will be pink in bad weather and blue in nice weather.

Weather - Clouds
Clouds are made of water. When they get too wet or full of water, it rains. Illustrate with a sponge. It will hold the water for awhile, but when it gets too full, it rains out.

Weather - Thermometers
Have the children note that the longer the line is on the thermometer, the warmer it is. Using two thermometers, have the children note where it is warmer, inside or outside.

Water - Evaporation
Put water in a jar and mark the water level. Let it stand. After a week, note the decreased water level.

Water - Condensation
Put cold water in a glass. Add ice cubes. Moisture will form on the outside of the glass. Explain that moisture in the air "condensed" on the glass, going from a gas state to a liquid state.

Water - It Conforms to Its Container
Have containers of all different shapes. Pour water from one container to another. Note if it looks like more or less. Also, note that the water was one shape in one container and another shape in another container.

Water - Pop Bottle Musical Pitches
Fill pop bottles of the same size with various amounts of water. Tap the bottles with a pencil and note the differences in pitch. Play a melody.

Water - Its Sound
Note the pouring sounds that are made while filling containers of different sizes and shapes with water. Also, tap them with a pencil while empty and when full.

Water - Sidewalk Painting
Have the children paint on the sidewalk with water. Later have them observe that the water evaporated.

Water - Wet and Dry Things
Have the children feel a cracker, a noodle, and paper. Then put each in a separate cup of water. Let the children feel them again a half hour after.

Water - Warm to Cool
Give each child a small paper cup of warm water. Have him/her taste it. Then add an ice cube to each cup. In a minute have the children taste the water again. It should be cooler.

Water - Weighing It
Weigh two sponges of the same size on a balance scale. They should balance. Next soak one in water. Then weigh them again, comparing the wet one to the dry one.

Water - Float or Sink
Have a dishpan of water and objects for the children to set in the water to find out if they float or sink.

Water - Colors
Mix food coloring in the primary colors red, blue, and yellow with water in baby food jars. With an eye dropper, mix the colors in a fourth jar to make new colors. For each mixture use another jar.

Water - Snow and Salt
Have two pans of snow of the same amount. Sprinkle one with salt. Observe which melts the fastest.

Water - Snow
Have a tray of snow for the children to observe with a magnifying glass.

Water - Icicles
Bring in icicles in a pan. Observe what happens to them.

Water - Great Ice Cube Race
Give each child an ice cube of the same size in a paper cup on which his or her name is written. Instruct the children to place their cups where they think the ice will melt the fastest. Note which ice cube melts first.

Stones - Rock Scratch
Scratch a rock with a nail. With a magnifying glass, examine the scratch and particles that were scratched from the rock. Compare particles to sand.

Stones - Weight Comparison
Compare the weight of various stones by placing them on a balance scale.

Stones - Collection
Have the children collect many different kinds of stones. Compare them to those in books or rock collections. Identify and name them when possible.

Stones - Categorizing
Categorize stones by size, shape or color.

Air - Fire Needs Air
Place an inverted glass over a lighted candle. It will burn until the air is used up. At the same time burn another candle, but do not put a glass over it. Note that the second candle continues to burn because it has more air.

Air - Air in Solutions
Use a commercially made bubble solution or dish soap and drinking straws to blow bubbles. Note that the bubbles are made when air is blown into the bubble solution.

Air - Paper Airplanes
Make paper airplanes and fly them. Observe that they do not fall immediately and that the air is holding them up.

Air - Escaping Air
Inflate a balloon, tie it and measure its circumference. Set it in a refrigerator for a half hour. Then measure again. Measure with a string both times, marking its circumference.

Air - It Takes Up Space
Show the children a balloon. Show them that it can fit in a very small box. Blow it up and then try to put it in the same space. Ask the children why it will not fit. Point out that air was the only thing put into it.

Air - It Causes Movement
Blow on a pinwheel. It moves without you touching it. Notice how the wind moves things such as clouds and leaves.

Air - Supports Weight
Demonstrate that most things fall when dropped. However, ask the children to name some things that do not fall when in the air (airplanes, jets, hot air balloons, blimps, helium balloons, kites, hang gliders, bugs, birds.) Also, fly a kite outside to show that air holds the kite up.

Air - Particles in the Air
Spread vaseline on a piece of paper. Attach the paper to a wall. Leave in place for several days. Observe all the particles that stick to it which were floating around in the air.

Plants - Planting Seeds
Plant seeds in two containers of soil. Water one but not the other. Note how the plants fare.

Plants - Planting Seeds
Plant seeds in two containers of soil. Place one in a closet and one in the sunshine. Note that both will come up. Put them back in the same locations. See which continues to grow.

Plants - Rooting Leaves
Place stems of leaves such as philodendron in water. Watch the roots grow.

Plants - Fruit Seeds
Cut fruits such as apple, pear, grape, banana, or a tomato in half. Take out some of the seeds from each. Let the children examine the seeds in and out of the fruit. Have a magnifying glass available.

Plants - Indian Corn
Have Indian corn (husk, cob and kernels) on the science table for the children to examine with a magnifying glass.

Plants - Mold
Place a slightly dampened slice of bread in one sandwich bag. In another place some grapes. Put both bags in a warm, dark place for a few days. Then, check for mold. Replace them for another week. Then have the children examine the contents with a magnifying glass. Explain that molds are plants even though they do not come from seeds, are not green and do not have flowers.

Animals - Bird Nests
Bring in an abandoned bird nest for the children to observe. Note what it is made from. Talk about how the bird put it together.

Animals - Cocoons
Bring a cocoon in on a branch and place it in a glass jar with holes punched in the cover. It may develop into a butterfly.

Weight - It Holds Things
Have two identical cereal boxes. In the bottom corner of one place a large enough amount of clay to balance the box while it hangs over the edge of a table. Show how one box stays on while the other falls off. Ask the children why one stays on. Then show them what is in the box to keep it on.

Weight - Weight Boxes
Use three identical boxes. Place cotton in one, plaster of paris in the second, and nothing in the third. Have the children compare the boxes' weights by lifting them and weighing them on the balance scale.

Magnets
Place magnets on the science table along with some objects that are and others that are not attracted by the magnets. Have the children experiment to see which are attracted by the magnets.

Magnets - Paper Clips
Have magnets of different sizes and strengths on the science table along with several dozen paper clips. Have the children see how many paper clips each magnet will pick up.

Shaker Container

Place styrofoam pieces in a shaker container. Have the children guess what is in it. Do the same with jingle bells, rice, pennies, and water. Also, use other contents for more variety.

Sniffing Bottles

Place some ground coffee in a small jar. Have the children smell it and tell you what it is. Do the same with peppermint, orange, cinnamon sticks, lemon, peanut butter, and cologne. Also, use other contents for more variety.

Feel Box

Place an apple in a box. Cover the box with a lid which has a hole large enough for a child's hand to reach through. Have the children feel in the box and guess what they feel. Do the same with feathers, marbles, keys, and stones. Also, use other contents for more variety.

Chemical - Secret Ink

Using a fountain pen (or other pointed object), write a message in lemon juice on plain white paper. Place the paper on a light bulb to reveal the message.

Chemicals - Crystals

To a jar half filled with water, add salt, one tablespoon at a time. Stir constantly each time. Stop adding salt when it no longer dissolves. Then, tie string to a stick that will span the top of the jar. Also, tie a washer to the other end of the string. Dangle the string down into the jar (using the washer to keep the string down and the stick to keep it from falling in). Crystals will form on the string. To grow larger crystals, place the jar in a warm, quiet place.

F. GAMES

Children enjoy games. While they may tend to play familiar ones over and over, on occasion, they like to learn new ones. An ever expanding game file is a must for the preschool classroom.

==
Games
==

[Select each day's games in advance and note them on your daily lesson plans. You may wish to copy them and glue them onto index cards.]

Ball Game

The children sit in a circle. The child holding the ball says, "My name is _____" and then rolls the ball to someone else. The child who catches the ball repeats the process. Continue until all the children have been included.

Skating to Music

The children remove their shoes and slide their stocking feet on a smooth floor such as linoleum. They skate in rhythm to the music. Choose music appropriate for ice skating such as waltzes or polkas with winter subjects.

Doggie Doggie

The children sit in a circle. One child walks around the outside of the circle and places a bone behind another one of the children while the group covers their eyes and says, "Doggie, doggie, where's your bone? Hurry up and bring it home." Then the children turn around to see if the bone is behind them. The one with the bone (receiver) tries to catch the one who put it there (giver) before he runs around the circle and gets in the receiver's spot. If the giver gets to the receiver's spot without being caught, the receiver takes a turn, placing the bone behind another child. If the receiver catches the giver, the giver takes another turn. Continue until all have been included.

Bean Bag Toss

- The children toss bean bags to each other, improving their motor skills at the same time.

- The children may also do this standing in a circle. The child holding the bean bag gives personal information or discusses a topic, then tosses the bag to another child, who does the same.

- Bean bags may be tossed through holes cut in stiff cardboard or a wooden board.

- Bean bags may be tossed to marks on the floor.

Hot Potato

The children sit in a circle. While music is being played, the children quickly pass around an object (such as a ball) representing a potato. When the music stops, they stop passing it. The child holding the hot potato quickly tosses it into a clothes basket which is in the middle of the circle. When the music starts, the leader gives the hot potato to a child who starts passing it around again.

Paper Snowballs

- Have each child wad up a sheet of white paper. The children then take turns tossing the "snowballs" into a wastebasket or clothes basket.

- The paper may be glued together to make a snowman.

- Have the children use their imaginations as to what to do with the snowballs.

[Note: You may want to avoid the chaos a snowball fight can cause.]

The Chickens and the Fox

Divide the room into thirds. Chicks stand in the first section, a fox in the second section and a mother hen in the third. The mother hen says, "Little chicks, little chicks, won't you come home?" The chicks say, "We can't because the fox will get us. "The mother hen says, "Come home anyway." The chicks run to the mother hen. The fox touches as many chicks as possible. The ones touched are now foxes and they help catch the chicks. The mother hen goes to the first section and calls to the chicks. Continue until all are caught. The last one caught becomes the fox for the next game.

Charlie Over the Water

The children form a circle with one in the middle. All sing: "Charlie over the water. Charlie over the sea. Charlie catch a blackbird, can't catch me." At the end of the song, everyone stoops. The person in the middle tries to touch someone before he stoops. Choose another child to be Charlie and continue the game.

Did You Ever See a Lassie

The children stand in a circle with a girl in the middle going through an action such as hopping. The group sings: "Did you ever see a lassie, a lassie, a lassie? Did you ever see a lassie go this way and that? Go this way and that way, go this way and that way. Did you ever see a lassie go this way and that?" The child in the middle decides on the action and those in the circle follow. Discuss possible actions before beginning the game. Also be ready to give suggestions during the game. Use "laddie" when it is a boy's turn.

Musical Chairs

Place a happy face picture on one chair. The children walk around chairs (one for each child) while the music is playing. When it stops, they quickly sit down. The one who sits on the happy face picture has to give a big smile. Move the picture and continue the game without eliminating anyone.

Bear Hunt

Act out the following: Let's go on a Bear Hunt. You'll have to be brave and strong. Let's go. Hurry! Open the door. Shut the door. Climb this tree. Swim the big river. Now go through tall grass. Look, there's a scary cave. Let's sneak up to the opening. Let's go inside. It's so dark in here I can't see anything. Shhhhh! I feel something furry. It's a bear! Let's get out of here! Go through the tall grass. Swim the big river. Climb the tree. Open the door. Shut the door. Whew! Safe at home.

Duck Duck Goose

The children sit in a circle. The child who is "it" walks around the outside of the circle saying "Duck" as he touches each child's head. When "it" says "Goose" while touching a child's head, that child runs after "it" who tries to get to that child's seat in the circle before being caught.

Curriculum Activity Selections

G. FIELD TRIPS

The number and nature of field trips for a class depends on many factors: local resources, adult supervisors, transportation, budget, insurance, the children's abilities and others. The following possibilities are both educational and of interest to most children.

Field Trip Suggestions

Airport	Farms	Library
Apple Orchard	- pumpkin	Maple Syrup Demonstration
Art Gallery	- horse	(or other food harvest)
Band Room	- cattle	Museum
Bank	- turkey	Nature Center
Bus Ride	- dairy	Parks
Children's Television Show	Fire Station	Planetarium
County Fair - animal exhibits	Hospital	Post Office
Favorite Eating Places	Ice Fishing Trip	Train Rides
		Zoo

H. BULLETIN BOARD IDEAS:

To stimulate the interest of the children, bulletin board displays should be changed often and be related to the themes and topics that are covered in the Daily Lesson Plans.

Bulletin Board Ideas

[Note: Prepare labels for each idea. Reuse them from year to year.]

School Acquaintance:

Country School House - Draw and cut out a school from red and black construction paper. Assemble on a bulletin board.

Fall:

Hand Print Tree - Draw trunk and branches of a tree on a large piece of paper. Have the children put their hands in red, orange, yellow, or green paint and then place their hands on the paper to make fall leaves. Write names by some of the leaves from each child.

Fall Scenes - Have the children pick out pictures of fall scenes from your picture file or from magazines. Place these pictures on the wall. (Do likewise for other seasons.)

Fall Picture - Enlarge a fall picture from a coloring book. Have all interested children color it. When finished, place on a wall.

Apple Tree - Draw an apple tree without apples on a large sheet of paper. All interested children may color it. Have each child cut out an apple shape, write his or her name on it (with help if necessary) to glue on the tree.

Turkey - Attach a turkey body (or bodies) without feathers onto a bulletin board. Have the children color some pre-cut feathers. Then, arrange the feathers in a fan and staple them to the turkey on the bulletin board.

Thanksgiving Collage - Gather magazine pictures of people of all ages, animals, toys, food, homes, clothing, plus anything else you think the children might be thankful for. Place a large sheet of paper on a wall. Write "We Are Thankful for Many Things" on it. Have each child choose picture(s) of things he or she is thankful for and glue the picture(s) onto the large sheet. Then have the child write his/her name (help if necessary) by the picture.

Teepee - Draw and cut out a teepee. Have all interested children color it. Then put it on the bulletin board.

Shapes:

Shape Man - Draw and cut geometric shapes out of different colors of construction paper. Assemble them on the bulletin board in the shape of a man.

Winter:

Doily Snowman - Make a snowman using lace doilies to make the circles. Add small doilies from the top of the middle circle to make arms. Add hat, facial features and buttons cut from construction paper. Add a scarf cut from fabric.

Stuffed Snowman - Staple together two large white paper circles leaving on opening. Stuff this circle with wadded up newspaper and staple it shut. Do the same with two medium-sized and two small-sized white paper circles. Staple these three stuffed circles together making a snowman. Paint or color on facial features, buttons, scarf, arms, and broom. Add a construction paper hat.

Snowflakes - 1. Fold square paper in half. 2. Now fold in thirds. 3. Cut across the top. Draw lines along the sides. Instruct the children to cut on the lines drawn on the paper being sure to keep the paper folded. Then he or she unfolds the paper to see the snowflakes.

Jobs:

Collage of Occupations - Cut out pictures of people (young, old; male, female; all races) doing all kinds of jobs. Mount them on a large sheet of paper and put it on a wall or bulletin board.

Senses:

Collage of Senses - Cut eyes, noses, mouths, ears and hands out of magazine pictures. Have the children glue them on a large sheet of paper and put it on a wall or bulletin board.

Fabric Collage - Have the children glue varied textures of fabric on paper.

Family:

Family Member Collage - Have the children find and cut out magazine pictures of people to represent all family members (fathers, mothers, brothers, sisters, selves, babies, grandparents, aunts, uncles, cousins). Have them glue these onto a large piece of paper that will be hung on a wall. Talk about family members as you do this activity.

House - Draw and cut out a picture of a house with shutters and a door that can be folded open. Glue room settings from catalogs and magazines to be seen when the shutters and door are opened. Include a kitchen, a living room, a bedroom and a bathroom.

Address:

Map of the Children's Homes - Draw a large local map, including all the streets where the children live. Show the children where their houses are located. Have rectangles, squares and triangles available for the children to use to make houses. Then, put the finished houses on the map and write each child's name and address below his or her house. Display the map on a wall.

Telephone:

Telephone Collage - Have each child choose a picture of a telephone and glue it onto a large sheet of paper shaped like a telephone. Write each child's telephone number and name under the small picture that he or she chose. Display the large telephone on a wall or bulletin board.

Valentine's Day:

Valentine's Man - Using red, pink and white construction paper, draw and cut out the pieces for a Valentine's man.

Transportation:

Vehicle Collage - Have the children cut and glue magazine pictures of all types of vehicles onto a large sheet of paper. Display it on a wall or bulletin board.

Health:

Collage of Foods for Each of the Four Basic Food Groups—Divide a large sheet of paper into four equal parts. Title these sections "Dairy," "Fruits and Vegetables," "Meats," and "Bread and Cereal." Have the children cut out magazine pictures of food. Have the children glue on appropriate pictures working on one section at a time.

Spring:

March - "In Like a _____ / Out Like a _____," or Cut out a lion and a lamb from construction paper. Also, write "lion" and "lamb" on separate cards. Display the lamb and lion picture with their cards in the order that correctly describes the conditions for the year.

Butterfly - Have all interested children paint a large butterfly (enlarged from a coloring book drawing). Display on a wall when dry. Also, display many smaller butterflies on the walls around the room.

Flower Garden - Draw leaves and stems on a long sheet of paper. Have the children color in the flowers.

Kites - Draw kites on various colors of construction paper. Have the children cut them out and decorate them. Add string and tails and display them on a bulletin board, wall or ceiling.

April Fool - Enlarge an April Fool figure and place it on a bulletin board with a tack in its middle to allow it to be turned.

Dot-to-Dot Chick - All interested children take turns connecting the dots on a chick (enlarged from a coloring book picture). Then, have them take turns painting the picture. When dry, display it on a wall.

Bunny - Draw, color, and cut out. Place on bulletin board.

Day and Night:

Day and Night Mural - Place a large sheet of black paper next to the same size of white paper. Then, have the children draw pictures on the papers to show what they do during the night and the day. Have them use chalk on the black paper and crayons or markers on the white paper.

Farm:

Barn Collage - Cut out pictures of barns from magazines. Have the children use them to make a collage on a large sheet of paper. Display it on a wall.

Farm Animal Collage - Have the children glue pictures of farm animals on a large sheet of paper.

Animals:

Animals - Large Picture of a Zebra - On a large of paper, draw a picture of a zebra enlarged from a coloring book. Have the children paint in black stripes. Display on a wall when dry.

Zoo Animals - Have the children draw pictures of zoo animals on paper the same size paper as the cages (that have been cut out in advance). Have the children glue the cages over their animals. Label these with the animals' names and put them in a row on a bulletin board or wall.

Water Animal Collage - Draw a pond on a large sheet of paper. Cut out pictures of water animals and glue them on that sheet of paper. Put it on a bulletin board or wall.

May Day:

Maypole - Draw on large paper and place on bulletin board. Use yarn for lengths of maypole ribbon.

Music:

Collage of Musical Instruments—Cut out pictures of musical instruments and glue them on a large sheet of paper. Put this on a bulletin board or wall. The pictures may be from magazines, catalogs, or coloring books.

5

PROGRAM MANAGEMENT AIDS

The aids found in this chapter keep the preschool program manageable. The checklists make it possible to keep track of, and report on, the children's progress through the school year.

This chapter details which files to make in order to organize information about the children, to have a place for material related to the themes in the Daily Lesson Plans and to maintain other categories useful in operating a preschool.

Another important aspect covered in this chapter is parental involvement which is of great importance to a child's success.

A. CHECKLISTS

The purpose of the following checklists is to give an organized, written overview of the children's skill in various developmental areas.

1. Intellectual/Physical Development

By following the 67 Daily Lesson Plans, all Lesson Objectives on the checklist will be covered. Some lessons are presented three times (in three variations) throughout the 67 plans (to show a child's progress and development). Therefore, they are listed three times on the checklists.

This checklist may be kept in a file folder or in an notebook, whichever is more convenient. To add more names, tape a sheet along the right side of each page of the checklist. The additional sheets may be folded over the original checklist pages in order to fit into a notebook or file folder.

Record the success level of the children on these lesson checklists. A checkmark may be used to show that a lesson was completed. Codes may be used in a small square to show the children's success levels. Further notes can be made in the margins, on the back of the checklists or on another sheet of paper.

INTELLECTUAL/PHYSICAL DEVELOPMENT CHECKLIST

NAMES:

Skill: Language Development
Objective: To construct sentences using—

1) present tense verbs
2) past tense verbs
3) future tense verbs
4) "when" and "where" questions
5) "what" and "who" questions
6) "yes" and "no" questions
7) plural inflections
8) possessive form of names
9) negative in the middle
10) pronouns
11) adverbs
12) adjectives
13) conjunctions
14) relative clauses

Objective: To increase vocabulary by naming—

15) classroom objects
16) fall items
17) winter items
18) spring items
19) articles of clothing
20) edible objects
21) foods in the four basic food groups
22) family members

Objective: To learn directional terms—

23) up, down, around
24) on, off - in, out
25) front, back - in, on, between
26) top, bottom, sides - open, close

Program Management Aids

NAMES:

Objective: To increase listening comprehension through—

27) nonsense "yes" and "no" questions
28) riddles - Who am I? What am I?
29) hidden sound
30) environmental sounds
31) louder, softer sounds
32) xylophone patterns
33) opposites

Objective: To enhance correct word pronunciation by—

34) pronouncing initial sounds clearly
    pronouncing initial sounds clearly
    pronouncing initial sounds clearly
35) identifying words that rhyme
36) identifying words with same initial sounds
37) identifying words rhyming with name
38) identifying words with same initial sound as name

Skill: Memory
Objective: To recall data necessary to—

39) follow directions
    follow directions
    follow directions
40) repeat series of numbers and series of words
    repeat series of numbers and series of words
    repeat series of numbers and series of words
41) answer story questions
    answer story questions
    answer story questions
42) name colors
    name colors
    name colors
43) name body parts
    name body parts
    name body parts
44) sequence pictures

	NAMES:							

45) retell events
46) tell activities of preschool day
47) name days of the week
    name days of the week
    name days of the week

Skill: Math Readiness
Objective: To establish a basis for understanding math by —

48) sorting objects
49) sorting objects on a grid
50) matching corresponding objects (one to one)
51) matching objects by touch
52) matching objects of proportionate size
53) recalling an absent object
54) remembering order of objects
55) naming numbers to
    naming numbers to
    naming numbers to
56) counting objects to
    counting objects to
    counting objects to
57) comprehending permanence of number
58) thinking back to earlier states

Skill: Visual Discrimination
Objective: To perceive and express relationships of —

59) similarity - same, different
    size - large, medium, small
    taller, shorter
    longer, shorter
    bigger, smaller
60) placement - first, middle, last
    distance - near, far
61) states of matter - solid, liquid, gas
62) speed - fast, slow
63) quantities - more, less

Program Management Aids

NAMES:

64) copying patterns
65) classifying by sizes
   classifying by shapes
   classifying by colors
66) completing picture
67) realizing whole picture from partial view
68) identifying what does not belong in a picture
69) continuing dot patterns
70) finding hidden pictures
71) finding hidden shapes
72) reproducing triangle patterns
73) finding path on maze
74) joining things that go together
75) matching object to object
   matching object to picture
   matching picture to picture
76) matching shapes
   matching letter positions

Physical Development Checklist
Skill: Gross Motor Coordination
Objective: To improve large muscle abilities by—

77) running, skipping, jumping, hopping
   running, skipping, jumping, hopping
   running, skipping, jumping, hopping
78) throwing and catching a ball
   throwing and catching a ball
   throwing and catching a ball
79) alternating feet down steps
   alternating feet down steps
   alternating feet down steps
80) walking backwards, walking on balance board
   standing on each foot five seconds
   walking backwards, walking on balance board
   standing on each foot five seconds

	NAMES:								

    walking backwards, walking on balance board ___

    standing on each foot five seconds ___

Skill: Fine Motor Coordination
Objective: To improve small muscle abilities by—

  81) buttoning, tying a knot, tying a bow ___

       buttoning, tying a knot, tying a bow ___

       buttoning, tying a knot, tying a bow ___

  82) zipping, snapping ___

       zipping, snapping ___

       zipping, snapping ___

  83) cutting on straight and curved lines ___

       cutting on straight and curved lines ___

       cutting on straight and curved lines ___

  84) putting together puzzles (no. of pieces) ___

       putting together puzzles (no. of pieces) ___

       putting together puzzles (no. of pieces) ___

Skill: Visual Motor Coordination
Objective: To develop eye-hand coordination by—

  85) connecting dots on angular and curved line ___

       connecting dots on angular and curved line ___

       connecting dots on angular and curved line ___

  86) copying a square, a circle, a triangle ___

       copying a square, a circle, a triangle ___

       copying a square, a circle, a triangle ___

  87) writing name ___

       writing name ___

       writing name ___

  88) drawing a person ___

       drawing a person ___

       drawing a person ___

  89) using left to right and top to bottom progression ___

       using left to right and top to bottom progression ___

       using left to right and top to bottom progression ___

  90) completing spatial designs ___

Program Management Aids

2. **Checklist of Observations**

The Checklist of Observations features types of behaviors to note in a child's intellectual, physical, social and emotional development. The three spaces which follow each type of behavior are provided for marking observations (based on the anecdotal records) at the end of each trimester.

CHECKLIST OF OBSERVATIONS

Name_____

	First Tri-semester	Second Tri-semester	Third Tri-semester
Intellectual Development **Work Habits**			
Involves self in own and planned activities			
Finishes projects			
Works with reasonable speed and accuracy			
Concentrates on activities			
Adequate attention span in a group			
Adequate individual attention span			
Can write the following numbers			
Can write the following letters			
Can write the following words			
Physical Development **Health**			
Sees and hears well			
Attends preschool regularly			
Appears well and rested			
Is normally active			
Has normal height and weight			
Fine motor skills			
Pastes, colors, paints, cuts			
Manipulates objects with ease			
Does fingerplays			
Social Development			
Interaction with peers			

Leads and follows		
Takes turns		
Handles conflicts		
Accepts others		

Interaction with Teacher

Responds well to suggestions and directions		
Accepts authority with neither too much dependence or independence		
Respects rules of class		

Emotional Development

Talks to teacher and children		
Directs energy into constructive activities		
Controls emotions by expressing feelings in language or in some physically acceptable way		
Appears contented, interested, calm, happy, and independent		
Possesses a positive self image		

3. **Year End Report**

The "Year End Report" is a compilation of information about each child that has been recorded throughout the year. It consists of an Intellectual/Physical Development Form, the Checklist of Observations, anecdotal records, and samples of the child's work. From this information, recommendations can be custom-designed for each child.

The information needed for the Year End Intellectual and Physical Development Form is obtained from the Intellectual and Physical checklists. Comments after each objective consist of "yes" or "no," "usually," "sometimes," or "seldom," depending on the recorded observations of the child's performance. If explanations are needed, they may be written in the margins, on the back, or on another piece of paper.

Place a copy of each child's Checklist of Observations in the "Year End Report." Also, anecdotal records may be added to the "Year End Report" (either in their original or rewritten form).

Include papers of the child's work which show his/her skills, as well as the drawings of a person (which were done three times throughout the DLP).

Program Management Aids

YEAR END INTELLECTUAL/PHYSICAL DEVELOPMENT

Intellectual Development

Name _____   Date _____

Language Development
- Uses most sentence structures _____
- Can be understood by a stranger _____
- Has acquired sufficient vocabulary to communicate ideas _____
- Knows names of objects in groups _____
- Knows directional terms:
  up, down, around; over, under; on, off _____
- in, out; top, bottom, sides; open, close _____
- front, back; in, on, between _____

Listening Comprehension
- Answers questions _____
- Finds hidden sounds _____
- Recognizes environmental sounds _____
- Recognizes louder, softer sounds _____
- Recognizes higher, lower sounds _____
- States opposites _____

Word Pronunciation
- Pronounces initial sounds correctly _____
- Recognizes words that rhyme _____
- Recognizes words that start with the same sound _____
- Memory _____
- Follows two or three directions without reminders _____
- Repeats words and numbers _____
- Answers story questions _____
- Knows colors _____
- Names body parts _____
- Sequences pictures _____
- Retells events _____

Tells activities in preschool day _____

Knows day of the week _____

Math Readiness

    Sorts objects on a grid _____

    Matches corresponding objects (one to one) _____

    Matches objects by touch _____

    Matches objects of proportionate sizes _____

    Recalls an absent object _____

    Remembers order of objects _____

    Names numbers up to _____

    Counts objects up to _____

    Understands permanence of number _____

    Thinks back to earlier states _____

Visual Discrimination

Perceives and expresses relationships of —

    Similarity - same, different _____

    Sizes - large, medium, small; taller, shorter; longer, shorter; bigger, smaller _____

    Placements - first, middle, last _____

    Distance - near, far _____

    States of Matter - solid, liquid, gas _____

    Speed - fast, slow _____

    Quantity - more, less _____

    Copies pegboard patterns _____

    Classifies by size, shape, and color _____

    Completes partially drawn pictures _____

    Realizes whole pictures from partial view _____

    Identifies what does not belong in a picture _____

    Continues dot patterns _____

    Finds hidden pictures and shapes _____

    Reproduces triangle patterns _____

    Finds path on maze _____

    Joins things that go together _____

    Matches object to object _____

    Matches object to picture _____

    Matches picture to picture _____

Matches shapes _____

Matches letter positions _____

Physical Development

Gross Motor Coordination

    Runs, jumps, hops, skips _____

    Throws and catches a ball _____

    Alternates feet walking down steps _____

    Walks backwards _____

    Walks on a balance board _____

    Stands on each foot five seconds _____

Fine Motor Coordination

    Buttons, ties knots, ties bows, zips, snaps _____

    Cuts straight and curved lines _____

    Puts puzzles together (no. of pieces) _____

Visual Motor Coordination

    Connects dots on angular and curved lines _____

    Copies square, circle, triangle _____

    Writes name _____

    Draws a person _____

    Uses left to right progression _____

    Uses top to bottom progression _____

    Completes spatial designs _____

B. RECORD KEEPING

Keeping accurate information, readily accessible, is an important part of preschool program management.

1. Child Information Form

When filled in, this form contains basic, current background information about each child in the class. This information should be kept on hand at all times, even on field trips. In cases of emergency, the Child Information Form provides specific information to facilitate quick parent (or guardian) contact. In less critical times, this information is also helpful for class lessons about learning addresses, phone numbers, and family names.

CHILD INFORMATION FORM

Child's Name (Last)_____ (First)_____ (Middle)_____

Address_____

Phone _____ Birth Date _____ Age_____ Sex _____

Father's Name_____ Father's Employer Phone _____

Mother's Name_____ Mother's Employer Phone _____

Person to be notified in case of emergency other than parents:

Name_____

Address_____

Phone_____ Relationship_____

Names of persons other than parents to whom child may be released:

1._____ 2._____

3._____ 4._____

Child's Doctor_____

Doctor's Address_____

Phone _____

_____
Signature of Parent or Guardian

Date_____

Program Management Aids 135

2. Anecdotal Record Form

A written record of typical and/or unusual behavior patterns, both positive and negative (if any), should be kept for each child, from the start of the school year.

For ease of access, anecdotal records should be filed together, rather than in individual files. Date every entry that is made. During each period of the day, throughout the day, observe two children closely. Note with whom they play, what they do, and the things they like or dislike. Observe their feelings (both expressed and acted out). Continue by observing two more children the next day, until all of the children have had a turn being observed and recorded, at which time start over again. Also, when any child exhibits noteworthy behavior at any time, be sure to record it.

ANECDOTAL RECORD FORM

Name:_____

Birth Date:_____

Date: / Anecdotal Observation

/

/

/

/

/

/

/

3. Attendance Charts

Make an attendance chart with the children's names and birth dates written in horizontal columns. Write the dates of the month at the tops of the vertical columns. Mark attendance each day.

4. **Individual Child File Folder**

Create and maintain an individual file for each child in the class. The file's contents should include:

— a current physical examination form which details immunizations. Be sure it is up to date.
— miscellaneous drawings and other papers done by the child showing his/her developmental level.
— correspondence from the child's parent/guardians (for future reference).
— questionnaire (see above) which contains information provided by the parents about their children to help you know them better and work with them more effectively.

5. **Resource Files**

The Teacher should keep a wide assortment of files filled with ideas and materials about the varied topics and themes that will be covered in the Daily Lesson Plans and other class activities.

a. **Theme-Related Files**

Every Daily Lesson Plan is centered on a particular theme. The following assortment of theme-related categories corresponds to the themes covered in this book's Daily Lesson Plans, plus some useful miscellaneous categories. Establish files to accommodate collected materials for each category.

THEME-RELATED CATEGORIES

Alphabet Pictures - pictures beginning with each letter of the alphabet	Animals	Holidays
	School Acquaintances	Telephones
People - babies and children	Day and Night	Explorers
People - young people, adults		
People - families and groups	Seasons - fall, winter, spring, summer	Health - food, water rest, exercise
Addresses - houses and rooms	Games - non-theme related	Family
Plants	Senses	Farm
Jobs	Shapes	Music
Toys	Stories - non-theme related	Transportation

b. **General Files**

Many additional categories of essential records and materials fall into this classification. Among them are:

— correspondence file
— master/original file (for all charts/forms)
— class photographs (individuals and group)
— budget
— form letter originals

C. Home/School Interactions

A preschool program is most effective when the parents and the teacher have positive interactions.

1. Parental Involvement in the Preschool Program

Parents are usually very willing to become active in the preschool program if they know what is involved and what is needed. Therefore, the preschool's activities and needs must be communicated to the parents through meetings, newsletters, personal notes, personal telephone calls and telephone call groups (prearranged message-forwarding contact groups).

A meeting of parents at the beginning of the year provides a great opportunity for the teacher to explain the school program and to let the parents know exactly how they can support their children.

A monthly newsletter will continue to convey the message as well as to inform its readers about timely items, such as the need for "scrounge" materials (items that might otherwise be thrown away) or theme-related pictures. Also, a monthly newsletter is useful for informing parents of field trips and special events for which drivers and/or additional helpers are needed. To enlist parental support, list the services and the dates that are needed in the monthly newsletter.

An even more direct approach can be achieved through writing personal notes to inform parents of their child's behavior and, if needed, a plan for its improvement. Personal notes are especially nice when used to praise children and to thank parents for their help or for having given materials.

Personal telephone calls can have the same results as personal notes and they have one obvious advantage — the teacher gets to hear the parent's response immediately which should result in better communication.

Telephone call groups can save the teacher time in relaying messages quickly to all the preschool families. The first step is to divide the families into groups of four or five. Next, the teacher should send lists with the names and telephone numbers of each group's members to every family in the group. As a result, when its necessary to make a quick communication with all of the families, the teacher can make a few calls (one to each group), and those people can relay the message to the other families in their groups.

In all of these forms of communication with parents, the teacher should encourage questions and comments. The better the communication exchange between the parents and the teacher, the better informed the teacher will be about the children and, therefore, the better prepared the teacher will be to promote the children's development.

Especially important in dealing with parents (or anyone who lends assistance or material support) is that the teacher should be generous with "thank you's" and whenever possible, express appreciation in writing.

2. Preschool Preparation

Before the start of school, parents should visit the school and received a list of suggested activities to help prepare their child to the soon-to-be-undertaken adventure of going to school.

The following list contains many valuable suggestions.

PRESCHOOL PREPARATION LIST

- Bring your child to school before the first day to acquaint him or her with the teacher and the school environment.

- Help your child understand the importance of preschool. Allow your child to stay home only when ill, not just when he or she feels like watching television or engaging in some other activity. Preschool is a place where the children will grow in all developmental areas, physical, social, emotional, and intellectual. Tell your child that he or she will learn, make and do many new things, and that he or she will meet other children and make new friends.

- Be sure your child has rested enough to go through the preschool session. The child is more apt to be successful if he or she is not tired.

- Breakfast or lunch before attending preschool gives your child necessary fuel for energy.

- Dress your child in comfortable play clothes to encourage active participation.

- Explain to your child that there will be many things for him or her to do and use, but he or she will have to "take turns" and "share." If these terms are unfamiliar to your child, demonstrate their meanings so he or she will begin to understand about getting along in a group.

- Reassure your child that his or her regular routine with a familiar caregiver will be resumed after school. Be sure your child knows what that regular routine will be if it changes when school starts.

- Discuss transportation arrangements with your child. If car pooling, have him/her meet the other drivers and their children before he/she will be picked up.

- Having your child take vision and hearing tests prior to preschool will assure you that your child sees and hears well.

- If your child has never been without you, make arrangements to leave him or her with friends or relatives for a short time. The child will learn that he or she will see you again. Gradually increase the length of time you are away from the child.

3. Questionnaire

At the beginning of (and throughout) the school year, the teacher will need to know certain specific pieces of information about each child in order to understand the child and help make his or her school experience both pleasant and beneficial. The following form should be filled in and returned to school by the parents of each child and then studied and kept ready to consult by the teacher.

PARENT BACKGROUND INFORMATION

Dear Parents,

Please return this sheet by mail or bring it to me at school. All answers will be kept confidential. They are intended to help me become better acquainted with your child and to assist me in planning activities.

1) By what name do you usually call your child? _____

2) Has your child any physical disabilities, including allergies, of which the preschool should be aware?

   If so, please explain. _____

3) What terminology does your child use to ask to go to the bathroom? _____

4) If your child has attended preschool before, was the experience enjoyable? _____

5) Does your child have tantrums? _____   Does he/she suck his/her thumb? _____

   If your child has unusual fears, what are they? _____

6) Does your child use the following at home? crayons____ scissors____ pencil____ chalk____ felt markers____

7) What would you like your child to gain from preschool? _____
   _____

8) Is there any area in which you anticipate difficulty for your child? (crafts, sharing, following directions?) ____

   If so, please explain. _____

9) What foods does your child like? _____

   What foods does your child dislike? _____

10) List any special interests your child has. _____
    _____

11) List names and ages of other children in your family. _____
    _____

12) Other comments you may have: _____
    _____

Thank you for your help in this matter.

Sincerely yours,

4. Learning Fun at Home

Parents and other family members are important partners in education. School and home working together is an unbeatable combination. The following note to parents and the list of suggested home activities are intended to reinforce classroom learning and fun at home activities.

a. Letter to Parents:

Dear Parents/Guardians:

Each day your child will come home with an assignment called "Learning Fun at Home." Completing this daily assignment is not mandatory and results need not be reported. Rather, the assignment is a suggested activity designed to reinforce some of the concepts and experiences that we are working on in school.

If you choose to do these daily activities with your child, please remember that it isn't necessary to complete every item. Also, be sure to praise your child's efforts as often as you can. It isn't necessary to follow every direction or to stick to an activity until it is completed. Even if your child should miss the whole point, be sure to find something about his or her performance to praise. Have fun with these assignments.

b. Daily Activities List for "Learning Fun at Home"

Each of these numbered activities corresponds with the numbered Daily Lesson Plan. In use, the activities should be separated into individual items, one for each day, and then duplicated to send a copy of each day's activity home with each child.

1) Have your child run, jump, then skip and then hop (first one, then the others) for a designated distance (such as from the house to you). If your child is not ready for all these activities, don't push. Show him or her how to do these activities and encourage him/her to try doing them.

2) Have your child use the puppet he/she made at school to tell what happened at preschool. To stimulate his/her memory, ask what he or she did during various activities such as the free play, art, story, snack, or lesson skill.

3) Draw a picture of a person as your child tells you what to draw. Draw only the body parts the child mentions.

4) Have your child write the first letter of his or her name. Write it first and guide his/her hand if necessary.

5) Have your child tell you the color of five different things.

6) Have your child tell you as many things as he or she can about a favorite animal.

7) Have your child write as much of his or her name as possible. Guide his/her hand in writing his/her name, if necessary.

8) Have your child gather some fall leaves and tell you about them. Topics may include colors, size comparisons, shape comparisons, where they were found, previous color, where they were before they fell on the ground, etc.

9) Have your child bring in two leaves and tell you in what ways they are alike and/or different.

10) Write each family member's name on a paper pumpkin. Have your child find his or her name.

11) Write the numbers 1, 2, 3, 4, 5 on a pumpkin. Help your child find his or her age on it and circle it.

12) Name an object in your home. Have your child name something that is bigger or smaller, taller or shorter, longer or shorter than what you named.

13) Hide a timer. Have your child find it by listening for its sound. Let him or her hide it for you to find.

14) Help your child to tie his or her shoe. Work on perfecting this skill for as long as you are both comfortable doing it. Shorter, more frequent sessions are in order for such a difficult skill.

15) Help your child snap and zip. Work on perfecting this skill for as long as you are both comfortable doing it.

16) Using the hikers made during art, have your child tell about their clothing and equipment. Also, how does his/her clothing differ from that of the hikers?

17) Name the days of the week. Have your child tell you what day it is. Give hints such as yesterday was _____, and go through the previous days. Talk about what day it will be tomorrow.

18) Put two different kinds of items (i.e., boats and blocks, more of one than another) on a flat surface. Have your child tell you or point to the group with more. Change the numbers of each item and have your child identify the group with less.

19-21) Have your child find all the objects he or she can that are circle shaped. Give him/her an example for a point of reference. Do the same with a square and a triangle.

22) Have your child make a circle and a triangle and then a square by forming his or her fingers into these shapes.

23) Have your child look in a mirror (full length if possible), and name as many body parts as he/she can.

24) Place four objects on a piece of paper. Have your child name them. When he or she is not looking, remove one and have him/her tell you which one was removed. Repeat several times. Then, let him/her remove objects for you to say which one was taken away.

25) Have your child describe objects in your home that are of interest to him/her. Encourage use of adjectives.

26) Help your child think of words that start with the same sound as his or her name. Give two choices, one that starts with the same sound and one that does not. Be sure to emphasize the initial sounds. 27)

Have your child tell or show where he or she wants to put his/her wreath made during art. Give guidelines if there are areas where you do not tape or tack pictures.

28) Have your child choose a book to "read" to you. Have him/her show you the pictures and tell you as much about them that he or she can.

29) Help your child learn to dress himself or herself for outside play. Learning this is an ongoing skill.

30) Using the "Book of Winter Clothing" made during art, have your child tell you on which part of his or her body the different articles of winter clothing are worn.

31) Have your child tell you what he or she does during the day, starting with getting out of bed.

32-42) Have your child find something green and point it out to you. Do the same with blue, gray, orange, yellow, brown, white, black, red, pink and purple items.

43) Show your child a one and a five dollar bill. Talk about the pictures on them. Have him or her tell you about the people and other details pictured on them.

44) Ask your child questions to help him or her think of ways to be safe: Walking - Where do you walk? Where do you cross the street? What do you do before crossing the street? Riding in a Car or Bus - Do you sit or stand? Should you fuss or argue? How noisy should you be? What can you do while riding?

45) Have your child tell you where he or she would like to travel or stay overnight; also, what he/she will need to take on the trip.

46) During one of your meals, place bowls of inedible objects on the table along with the edible. Have your child tell you which to eat.

47) One group at a time, talk about the four basic food groups: milk, eggs and meat, fruits and vegetables, breads and cereals. Discuss numerous selections in each group. Have your child choose a favorite food from each.

48) Discuss some routine you have for your child most days, such as what he or she does before bed. Have him or her tell this sequence of events.

49) Look for signs of spring: warm weather, buds on trees, sports, baby animals, plants, flowers, robins, etc.

50) Read a story to your child. Have him or her tell you the main characters and what happened.

51) Help your child think of an April Fool's joke to play on a family member.

52) Have your child say when he or she is "out" of and "in" the house and when he or she is "on" or "off" a chair.

53) Have your child tell you about the colors and designs on his or her potted plant made during art.

54) Give your child two or three simple directions such as "Close the door. Hang up your coat. Wash your hands." or "Give me a kiss. Put on your coat. Go outside." See how many directions he or she can follow without your having to repeat them.

55) If it is not too late for your child's bedtime, point out the moon and stars. Also, talk about what lights the out-of-doors during the day and what lights it during the night.

56) Ask your child what he or she would like to do on a farm.

57) Have your child look for footprints of any animal (farm animals if available.).

58) Have your child explain which farm animals he or she likes best.

59) Discuss animals in zoos. Working together, name as many as possible.

60) Have your child count the flowers that he or she brought home in the May basket.

61) Have your child put one spoon by each plate at the dinner table.

62) Have your child observe two different kinds of trees and tell how they are the same and how they are different.

63) Have your child point to the leaves, stem and blossom on a flower.

64) Place two pennies on a table and have your child count them. Cover them with a cloth and ask your child how many are under the cloth. Remove the cloth to verify. Then, continue with three pennies, four pennies, etc., as long as your child understands that the number stays the same under the cloth as when he or she counted them.

65) Clap a simple rhythm and have your child shake the same rhythm with the shaker that he/she made in school.

66) Listen to some music. Ask your child if it is fast or slow. Check when it obviously speeds up or slows down.

67) Have your child tell you specific things he/she liked at school.

Program Management Aids

D. OPERATING EXPENSES

To determine a budget for a preschool, it is necessary to make a list of the personnel, supplies, facilities, equipment and services that will be required to operate the school. Minimum tuition charges can be figured by dividing the total of the costs for services and supplies by the number of students who are to be enrolled in the school.

Salaries
    Teachers
    Helpers

Training
    Professional conferences
    Inservice training
    Professional books
      and subscriptions

Rent

Renovations

Food

Insurance

Telephone

Auditing

Consumable Supplies
    Pencils - fat
    Color pencils
    Felt markers
     - fine and thick
    Crayons
    Scissors
     - regular and lefties
    Paint
    Paper - white 8 1/2 x 11"
      construction paper
     (all colors)
    Cardboard (for mounting)
    Tagboard
      (for cutting patterns)
    Roll of tablecloth paper
    Pins
    Glue and/or paste
    Rubber cement
    Calendar
    Chalk
    Finger paint
    Finger paint paper
    Soap
    Facial tissue
    First aid supplies
    Toilet paper

Office Supplies
    Tape
    Pencils and pens
    Felt markers
    Scissors
    Ruler
    Notebook paper
    Notebook
    Typing paper
    Typewriter
    Rubber bands
    Paper clips
    Brads
    Hole reinforcers
    Tacks
    Stapler and staples
    3" x 5" cards
    String
    Dictionary
    Paper cutter

Indoor Equipment
    Puzzles
    Clay
    Storybooks
    Magnifying glass
    Thermometer
    Balancing scale
    Trucks and cars
    Clothespins and line
    Climbing bars
    Balance board
    Paint easel
    Paint brushes
    Drop cloth
    Tables
    Chairs
    Chalkboard
    Felt board
    Bulletin boards
    Blocks
    Record player and records
    Tape player and tapes
    Games

Dramatic Play
    Stove
    Refrigerator
    Sink
    Dishes
    Pans
    Large mirror
    Dress up clothes
    Dolls
    Doll clothing
    Bed
    Blankets

Woodworking
    Saws (2)
    Hammers (2)
    Vice
    Drill
    Scrap lumber
    Nails
    Work bench
    Safety glasses

Rhythm Instruments
    Bells
    Cymbals
    Drums
    Rhythm sticks
    Sound blocks

Outdoor Equipment
    Swings
    Slide
    Teeter totter
    Climbing bars
    Jump ropes
    Sandbox,
      sand and sand toys
    Balls
    Trucks and cars
    Clothespins and line
    Outside games